VOLUM

Anonymous, beautiful and sometimes heart-wrenching stories from people just like you and me.

Jordan Corcoran

Listen, Lucy. Volume 1

By: Jordan Corcoran

To contact the author please visit: www.ListenLucy.org.

Printed in the United States of America

ISBN-10: 194413400X

ISBN-13: 978-1-944134-00-6

Dedication:

For Hazel Rose and Hudson.

You are my inspiration to continue to try

and create a better, brighter and more accepting world

where you can grow up and be exactly who you want to be.

Introduction

There are times in my life that I think back to and cringe. Times when my anxiety disorders consumed me. There are things I have said, reactions I have had, and ways that I have treated people that make me sick to my stomach. Those times still haunt me every once in a while. They remind me that I was never, and will never be, perfect and that I always need to be working on myself.

There are also times in my life that have made me cry. Times where the anxiety is all I could focus on. Defeat was all I felt. Times that I felt so alone and frustrated that all I could do was sob. Times where I looked in the mirror and thought to myself, "Who are you and how did you become so weak?" These times remind me where I came from and that I shouldn't take my health and happiness for granted for one minute.

There are some times in my life that give me chills. Times where the things I worked for, hoped for, and dreamed of became realities. The time I made the winning shot in my seventh grade basketball game against St. Mary's, when I published my first article in my college newspaper, walking down the aisle on my wedding day, jumping off of a cliff into the ocean in Jamaica, and launching *Listen, Lucy* for the world to see are all moments that make the hair stand up on my arms. These moments remind me that I am alive and that life is good.

Then there are moments of my life that I think of which fill me with triumph. Moments where all of those other experiences came together—the good, the bad, and the ugly—and helped me find my purpose. Telling my husband and family about *Listen, Lucy*, receiving my first story in my inbox, getting my photo taken with each group after I speak, my re-launch party, and this beautiful book are all moments I have worked to create. They give purpose and meaning to the struggle I face. It has made me realize that all of those other moments have formed who I am and the message I am spreading to the world.

The book you are about to read will make you cringe, cry, give you chills and fill you with triumph. It will also help you heal. This book is full of stories of people who have chosen to not be identified, but that need their stories to be heard. There are also some of my stories in here as well. I have signed my name at the end of my stories to let you all know it is important for me to not only talk the talk, but walk the walk. This book is full of stories of beautiful, brave, heart-wrenching moments of people's lives that, when combined together, create a message of struggle, strength, hope and togetherness. My hope is that when these courageous writers work through their struggles, they look back on the different moments of their lives and are able to create their own message to the world. I feel honored to have read these stories and to have the opportunity to share them with the world.

Thank you for listening, being there and supporting this movement.

DISCLAIMER

With no limitations and no editing, these stories show an unfiltered glimpse of what people are going through every day. These unidentified, courageous authors share their stories with the hope of letting go of what is weighing them down.

Listen Lucy,

I worry. A lot.

Some days more than others. Most days for little reason.

My worry derives anxiety. My anxiety, fear.

I have the tendency to overanalyze every little detail this fantastic, yet fickle life has to offer. I will read this piece 50 times over before I am comfortable submitting it.

I place more value on pleasing others than myself. I care more about how others perceive me than how I perceive myself.

I mask my emotions and insecurities with humor, wit and satire. I surround myself in a cocoon of materialism and aesthetics because it is a means of healing. I self-loath.

I worry about the future. I focus so much on the things I can't control and abandon the things that I can.

I am flawed.

I am aware of my flaws. I accept my flaws.

I am sure that many of your authors can draw parallels sto how I feel. I want them to know they are not alone. I think acknowledging what makes us imperfect is the first step to perfecting our imperfections. Someone once told me you will never love anyone until you first learn to love yourself.

No one is perfect. No one thing is perfect. But the process, the journey, the steps we take every day to better ourselves and those around us are what make the imperfections worthwhile.

We are often asked in this world to look a certain way. Act like this. Wear that. We are told to measure our success and failures against our peers. Society wants us to be the best looking, wealthiest, funniest, healthiest, He or She we can. Don't do you, Out do you.

Be Famous. Be Known. Be Great.

I Challenge You:

Be Yourself. Accept Yourself. Love Yourself.

I remember participating in a lot of sports growing up. I vividly remember a particular coach saying, "There is always someone out there outworking you as we speak" "You do 30 pushups this afternoon. There is someone out there doing 40" "You run 4 miles this morning. There is someone out there running 5"I think this general concept of thought is powerful and can be used to remind ourselves what we have in our lives.

I hate my job. I can promise you there is someone out there without employment. I can't stand my Mom. I can promise you there is someone out there without a Mother. I am losing my health. I can promise you there is someone who has days left on this earth. Abraham Lincoln said, "If we magnified our blessings the way we magnify our disappointments, we'd all be a lot happier."

Recognize your flaws. Embrace your flaws. Enjoy your journey.

I don't dismiss those whose situations seem without reclamation. Those who have hit rock bottom with seemingly no light at the end of their tunnel. It is easy to sit behind a computer and encourage others to stay positive in the face of adversity, but it is another thing entirely to have to live it every day.

I encourage those who have lost hope in the good this world has to offer and struggle to find the positive within their personal battles to trust in the power of each other. Lean on those around you. Reach out for help. Be a beneficiary of the world's love.

In turn, be a beacon of kindness for others. If we go out of our way to spread love and kindness to everyone we interact with each day we can make a difference in the lives of those who have lost faith and ultimately put their deepest and darkest days behind them.

Thank you for allowing me to share my flaws.

Continue to learn to accept yours.

Keep spreading the good vibrations.

Listen, Lucy,

So lately I just don't know what makes me happy. I have been mildly depressed since 10th grade. Now im 22 and it isn't getting any better. I see a therapist when I am at school weekly and she is amazing. (Side note: I recommend therapy for everyone because there is something about talking to someone, who only has your best interest in mind while still being a completely neutral person, that is just incredible.) I normally think that when I come home I feel better because my family is a huge support system for me. But now, even that doesn't seem like enough. I have friends but none of them really seem to understand or want to understand what is going on with me. It is hard being someone who would rather stay inside on a friday or saturday night and curl up in a ball because just the thought of seeing people, having to look cute, attract guys, and pretend like I am having the night of my life just exhausts me.

I am tired all the time. I am tired about thinking about being tired. I have a job, I do well in school, and I love what I study, and I'm a well-liked person. Most people think that should be enough...but it isn't. I am not happy, I am not excited, and I am never not tired. I just want to be someone who enjoys being social. I want to feel like I am attractive. I want to feel like I can be happy. Most importantly I want to feel like myself. I can't remember the last time I felt like myself lately. The worst part is that I never feel completely honest with myself or anyone really. I feel like I am constantly pretending and if I do start to try to open up to people I can't seem to let myself be honest with them either. I guess I don't trust that they will understand or want to hear what's going on with me. I don't even think I want to hear what they have to say or think about me because I don't ever think it will be what I need to hear.

The problem is, do those words even exist? What do you say to someone who feels completely alone in her thoughts and feelings and emotions. What do you say to someone who really has no real valid reason to feel the way she feels? I'm not looking for sympathy or a validation of my feelings. I know that my feelings are real and they don't have to be validated by anyone or anything. I know that I have people who love me. I guess what I really just need is someone real, in my life currently, to say that it is okay to feel how I feel. I need my friends to understand why I need to stay in on a weekend rather than go out and party. I need to be allowed to not feel guilty for my thoughts and emotions. I need someone to just say it is okay, and to respect however long of a time that takes me to feel happy again.

Today, I had the *Listen, Lucy* site up in the background as I prepared to organize things but as I tried to work on my to-do list, I felt like I couldn't focus. My thoughts were getting jumbled; I started to feel anxious and insecure. I started to sweat, I felt like I was going to cry and I couldn't figure out what was making me feel like this. I got out my journal and started to write out how I feel. I wrote about how my anxiety has been a real struggle for me over the past week and that I haven't felt this bad in a very long time. I explained what it felt like physically and what was happening mentally and that there was no big incident that was making me feel this way—there was no cause. My anxiety had been looming over my head for a week now, making my days more difficult, less enjoyable, and creating a constant, neverending fight within my mind. Through writing this out, I came to a realization.

I am a person who is living with Generalized Anxiety Disorder and Panic Disorder, but I really only talk about the Panic Disorder. In some ways, describing my Panic Disorder and panic attacks is easier. There is a cause and there is a physical effect. There is an incident and an explosion. As difficult as it is to go through, it is easier for me to explain this to people. Generalized Anxiety Disorder is a different animal—at least for me. It is like this intense worry that sits in your stomach, your mind and your chest all day but you can't figure out what is wrong. You can't make it go away. It is the annoying, defeating side of my anxiety that can completely exhaust me until I am reduced to tears. It is the side of my anxiety that makes me want to curl up in a ball, close my eyes and wish I would fall asleep and wake up a different person. It is the anxiety that slowly rocks me to my core.

Even though it is a difficult thing for me to talk about, I wanted to share this because if someone is reading this and is experiencing the hell that is Generalized Anxiety—please know that I understand. I am currently experiencing the nagging, petty, all-consuming worry that sits in your gut until it doesn't. I am struggling with you. You aren't crazy. Please don't sink into that lonely feeling. If you don't let it control your life, neither will I. Talk about it, write about it, tell me about it if it helps you and know that we are all in this together.

Knowing that *Listen, Lucy* is creating a community of support and acceptance is beyond comforting to me on my off days—and do I have some off days! I want to always be a role model of tenacity and acceptance. I want to make sure people look at me and think that I am doing my best to be a strong, positive force in the world. I think in order to do that, it is important for me to admit when I am weak. Pure honesty is what makes *Listen, Lucy* unique. And, if I am being completely honest—I am still working on myself and my struggles every day and I never want to lead on that I have it figured out. I assure you that I do not. But what I do know is that hearing your stories, seeing your support, feeling your acceptance and love of me, each other and of yourselves is something that encourages me to continuously work on figuring it out.

Thank you all for being brave enough to tell your stories to help me continue to tell mine.

Jordan

Listen, Lucy,

I've been super stressed lately. My grandfather has recently not been doing well, and he has spent a lot of time suffering in the hospital. Also, my mom, who also happens to be my best friend and closest confidant, is having surgery to remove part of her breast that needs to be tested for cancer.

On top of everything else, IT'S FINALS!

I'm having a lot of trouble concentrating, and all I ever want to do is sleep. My boyfriend is so sweet and really understands me, but I feel like sometimes he doesn't know what to say or how to treat me when I feel upset about what's going on at home. I feel guilty, like I'm wasting his time or something when I'm crying or just need to vent. It's not his fault, he just hasn't had anything like this happen to him before.

Normally, I am so strong. I'm the rock... People come to me when they need help or someone to confide in... and now I'm the one looking for a hand to hold.

It's also really hard for me to tell other people how I'm feeling or why I'm upset. I think a lot of my friends see me as someone who can take on the world with no problem and that nothing can get me down. But I don't think they understand how I feel when I crawl into bed at night and can't sleep because I'm so overwhelmed with the things going on in my life. I start to sweat and shake and cry because I know that when I wake up the next day, anything can happen... and that scares me. It scares me that I might not do well in school. It scares me that my grandfather could die at any moment. It really really really scares me that my mom could face the terrors of cancer. Most of all, though, it scares me that I, the strong rock that so many people depend on, am so scared.

Listen, Lucy,

Since I was in the 8th grade I have struggled with depression and anxiety. I am now a senior and still struggle. For a while I had myself convinced I was okay and that I would never get that bad again, well I was wrong, very wrong. This year I for lack of a better word relapsed, I cut again, and began to struggle more with being just sad all the time. Most days I feel like I'm stuck in my own head. Like I'm stuck in a really long nightmare almost. I do not attend regular school because of my issues. A lot of people these days try to romanticize depression and anxiety, those are the people who have never had to deal with being stuck in their own head, seemingly with no way out. They have never had to deal with feeling like the only way out is not being around anymore. Lately, I've been hanging on to a tiny strand of hope. Hope to get better. Hope to not feel like this anymore. Although, I have this tiny strand of hope, a lot of times; I feel like it's breaking.

Listen, Lucy

I always told myself that I wouldn't be affected by any sort of emotional scars. After 2 years of dealing with a chronic back problem that led to a rotator cuff injury, I was done. I told myself I'd take on a hard outer shell and only feel pain from physical injuries - because it made sense. You can feel it physically affecting you, everything hurts all the time.

I was pretty good at that, ignoring my emotions. The rest of my life was still together. I was in my senior year of high school and getting healed. I planned on playing water polo in college, and I thought I was healthy enough. And I was. My back was in good condition. I played the first semester, and in the second, something happened one day and my upper back and shoulders were injured. This was February of last year, 2014. I stopped playing sports and I lost my motivation for schoolwork, getting the lowest GPA I never thought I'd get. My parents were mad. Without playing sports, I had so much time to do stuff that I ended up doing nothing.

Over the summer I worked on my injury and got better. I was strong. I was lifting in the gym, swimming every day, and my muscles were getting stronger. I felt good. I came back to school and within the first week of sitting in classes my back was in so much pain. I went to one water polo practice and knew I had to stop. I started seeing doctors. I went to physical therapy at the student center, saw a sports medicine doctor, got an MRI for my neck, an EMG for my shoulder/right arm to check my nerves, saw physical therapy in the UPMC system. It seemed hopeless.

I was going to the gym every day though, lifting with 2 pound weights and feeling disgustingly embarrassed. No!! You don't understand!! I'm just injured! I'm strong! I wanted to shout at everyone but I couldn't. That's weird.

Second semester came and I was still in pain. I went back to physical therapy. I broke down crying at the gym and my friend had to come comfort me and tell me that I needed to stop going to the gym because I definitely wasn't strong enough. I cried at the end of classes when it hurt. I cried in front of people a lot. Think about feeling a pinching, pulling pain in your shoulder blades when you breathe. Think about leaning your head forward and feeling a disgusting pulling sensation in your upper spine in your muscles. Think about waking up and having your fingers numb from your nerves being impinged. Nerve pain isn't something you can massage out or ice away. Your shoulders hurt. It hurts to lift things. And then your doctor tells you he's disappointed in you because you aren't getting better. Your lower back is so sore when you wake up in the morning. It's a dull pain that just sits and settles. It's not something I'd wish upon anyone.

What people don't understand about physical pain, and what I only just realized is that it's a different type of stress on the body. So you have that, and then you get emotionally stressed and you get anxious and worried and you think you will never get better. And that's even more stress on your body. It's all so connected.

It's gotten to the point where I think every day if I should stay here. I could stop this pain so easily. It could just go away. But I can't do that because I need to show people that they can get through it. I'm not ashamed of going to counseling and seeing therapists and acknowledging that I have a problem.

I get embarrassed because people stare at me when I'm stretching in class. How amateur is that? I stand up to stretch my hips, I stretch my neck, my arms, and I just look like a complete doofus. Stop staring at me. STOP STARING AT ME I don't want this either! I don't want to feel like this!! Stop making me remember that there's something wrong with me. When I called the on-call counselor she told me that it's not me. You know what, people are just looking for a distraction. They're just curious. And if anything, I'm setting an example for people on how to be healthy.

Then I'm having problems with my friends, boys, feeling like I still need to lose weight to look better and make my back feel better, not getting good grades, having people compete with me to get good grades - I'm only there so they can feel better about having a higher grade than me, which isn't that hard anyway. My friend group is falling apart, I know things I shouldn't know and I'm losing my faith in some of them. I have so much stress on me to do my jobs perfectly in my sorority. I don't know how to say no to people and I take on too much. 12 credits feels like 12000 to me right now. I am so behind. I can't sit for 4 hours like people can in the library. I'm getting angry all the time. I scream, I yell, I act like I'm 2 years old when I'm 2 decades old. I get mad at everyone. And I'm so sorry. I wish I wouldn't.

I wonder if people think about how lucky they are. They can sit and study for hours and immerse themselves in the material. i'm always always thinking about my back. Always. What am I doing to make it better? Why does it hurt? They can push open those stupid revolving doors without wincing. They can do so much that I can't. I miss water polo, I miss being on a team. No one seems to understand what I am going through, and that's understandable. Only you will understand it all. But no one seems to be giving me a break. Oh, that's not a real problem. Your back just hurts. You're not in a cast, a sling, you didn't get surgery. Just suck it up, they say. How do I write excuses to my professors, my employers? I can't. I'm just stuck.

I scare myself into being in pain. I know I do. It's mental. So much of this is mental. It's scary how complex and amazing the human mind is.

My escape is playing guitar and thinking about soccer. When I play songs I forget that I'm in pain. I'm not that good but I like hearing my voice, it reminds me that I'm alive. When I watch soccer with people I'm reminded that this is a community that accepts you for who you are because you have one main goal in mind - watching soccer. It's like nothing I've experienced before. It makes me smile. It makes me happy and no one can take that away from me.

What am I doing next? I'm still going. I'm making these cheesy instagram posts everyday about positivity, good things in my life, and general deep things that should make people think. It's hard because I sometimes don't even believe it. Every time I start doubting my recovery, physically and mentally, I have to think of the post I make. That's keeping me here. I'm hoping that in some way I can inspire someone. Even if it's just one person, I've done my job. Laugh at me for being serious on social media, but this is me. I have to do this. I am breathing. I am working on my breathing because it makes me forget about my problems. For the time being.

My biggest fear is not being healthy enough to be an athletic trainer, which is all I've wanted in my life. For a year and a half, fine, but there's something about working with athletes who are driven, dedicated and committed every day. They inspire me so much. The discipline they have, that I need. I need to get better. There's no way around it. I'm scared of disappointing my parents with my grades, not being as good as my sisters at everything, being alone, and being stuck like this for the rest of my life.

My favorite quote is, "Run when you can, walk if you have to, crawl if you must, but never give up". I can't give up. I can't. I have to be here for other people who want to give up.

Instead of studying I'm spending half an hour typing this. I have a lab due on Thursday but I know that I need to clear my head. I am so scared of everything but I have to keep going. For my soccer team, for my friends, my family, and the future people that I can hopefully inspire. Thank you so much for listening.

Jordan, thank you so much for showing me that first of all, there are so many different types of things people go through. In the fact that we as humans struggle, I'm not alone. And that makes me feel good. I keep trying to put things in perspective. I'm not sure why I'm going to keep going but something in me tells me that it's all worth it. And that makes me feel good. Someone, if not me, can benefit from this. I don't think I can study any more tonight, but I have 2 tests next week on the same day and so much stuff to do. So much to do, so little time.

Listen, Lucy

They brought us to this country because they thought we wasn't equal. But little did we know slavery was only the prequel. We are going to talk about the persecution of black people. We can go back 300 years, 100 years, 50 years, 10 years! Every 8 hours a black body lays in the street. They never gave us a chance to compete. We was freed 1865. We thought the world couldn't be better. They never did like us. No matter how many black people they talk to in a day. Little boys used to want to be you. Now they wanna beat you.

Beat you that's what they do before they ask questions. Martese Johnson concealed in his own blood for all the wrong reasons. Apprehended by the police, broken, bloody and beaten. I'm getting scared about leaving the house. Don't wanna end up bleeding from my mouth. Tamir Rice maybe he still had hope in good cops. But all that hope died when they shot him nonstop. Media makes the black look darker. We try to make the black look brighter. They see us when we protest. Don't wanna meet us when we at our best. Becoming doctors, lawyers and teachers. But instead, they see us dead, in jail, or drug dealers.

My name is Aiyana Jones, I was 7 years old when the police broke down the front door and destroyed my home. I don't remember waking up from my dream that night. The pain I felt was slight. Then I felt nothing at all. I didn't get to say goodbye. It's unfair how they come and take. All the injustice built on our prayers & so-called mistakes.

I was asleep when I heard the screams and the gunshots that interrupted my dreams. My baby girl had goals, and a future. I keep going back to the time she was first born, 'cause instantly I fell in love. You never imagine having to bury your youngest, but for a black mother, that's your biggest fear. Burying them six feet under the ground while you can only watch through your tears.

And I can't help but wonder – does God truly see color? And if He can't recognize, then why can't our world be so colorblind? He watches as we gain frustration because of indignation, and does he not know that racists are hating because we all have a different pigmentation? Does God know that his creations are split apart in different nations, that careless racists are creating dangerous situations that will be passed down for generations? I know that God is colorblind. But even though He is, those who are not have no care for the lives of our kind.

Black Lives Matter. Black Lives Matter.

We Still Matter.

Listen, Lucy,

You visited and spoke to my class today and I thought your story was relatable. Currently, I am losing hope and I feel like I have no control over my life anymore. To start off, on Sunday my grandpa was diagnosed with lung cancer. He is going down fast and I know he doesn't have much longer. I am in high school and just this past year I started having panic attacks where they have caused me to quit a job and drop out of classes in school because I could hardly make it through the day. I am having severe anxiety over college and I feel like no matter what I do I won't be happy. I visited a college and had a panic attack there. I am staying overnight at one again this weekend so I am anxious about that. My mom made me start therapy for it, but I have seen little results. I am scared that I will not learn how to cope with my anxiety before the time comes that I have to commit to college or not, so I will not make the right decision. I am also in a long distance relationship that I don't know I should be in. We used to be really close and skype everyday but now we barely talk. It started when she told me that she doesn't want to skype everyday. I felt clingy so I backed off. She has only asked me to skype once since that a couple of months ago. She also has a lot of health problems and she says that I cause her stress and that is a threat to her health. I'm all for her being healthy obviously but she hangs out with friends and seems perfectly fine now. It's just frustrating because I thought she would be here for me. She was my only hope for getting through college and my anxiety. And now it's all in question. I feel like every choice I make I am going to regret it in one way or another and I am completely lost anymore.

Listen, Lucy,

I'd like to tell you a story - a story about a little boy that changed my life. I will call him Nick. I was paired to work with Nick at a summer program. I was fresh out of college and had my Elementary Education & Special Education degrees under my belt. Mo bosses warned me that Nick could be difficult to work with. Nick was seven years old and Nick was autistic. I hate to give him that label because he truly was like every other little boy at summer camp. He loved to swim, he loved to play ball, and he loved to swing on the swings. He hated art, but I am going to be honest with you, I hate art too. So Nick & I got along swimmingly. My first day with Nick is one that I will never forget. Our summer camp was located at a place that had a sweet playground. Nick LOVED the playground. Nick ran up to the playground and went straight for an innocent girl with blonde curls that was using the swing he wanted. He didn't know how to wait for his turn. He didn't know how to communicate what he wanted to me. So, he yanked her blonde curls and she shrieked. Her mother was mortified and immediately asked, "what is wrong with that kid?" I immediately grew angry. I took a deep breath and then I replied, "there is nothing wrong with him and we apologize that this happened, we are truly sorry". I will stand by my response until the day that I die. There is absolutely nothing wrong with Nick. God dealt Nick a different hand. His mother and I have discussed this many times. Nick cannot handle overstimulation. I can relate. Nick and I have never had a real conversation – this is a defining trait of autism. These amazing individuals are not the best communicators, they won't look you in the eye, they won't pick up on verbal cues, they will take everything you say extremely literal, and they will be the most exceptional, wonderful humans you will come across in your life. I hope you come across them. They will change your life and your outlook – just like they have for me. It took about a week for Nick to feel comfortable with me, for Nick to trust me. Just like it would with any new person in any child's life. At times, I would have to restrain Nick when he was uncontrollable. He loved it. I was giving him the biggest hugs and he loved hugs. My friends and family will tell you – I am not a hugger. But something about these hugs from this little man made my summer one that I will cherish forever and ever. There were days he would pee his pants on purpose because he did not want to hike up to the creek. Nick is a genius. He outsmarted me on many occasions. I loved it. I will never forget when Nick told me that he loved me, he said, "I love you, (insert my first & last name)". To this day, he calls me by my first & last name. He's seriously the coolest. He's grown up into an exceptional young man. He's doing so well. I couldn't be more proud. I get messages from his mom from time to time – they always have a simple message – Nick says, "I love you, (insert my first & last name)". The fact that he still talks about me to his family after all these years makes me smile from ear to ear.

When I think back to how unhealthy and unhappy and uncertain I was when I was nineteen, I wish I could tell myself, "Push through it. Stay focused. You definitely are not alone in this. In the end, you are going to do something really cool with all you are going through. Trust yourself."

Unfortunately, I can't go back in time to tell myself that—even if it would make it easier for me to handle everything. But, I can move forward in telling other people these thoughts and that is exactly what I plan to do.

I could never have dreamed of what *Listen, Lucy* would accomplish in under two years. Every day, I am blown away by the support I am shown and the beautiful content that I get to read and share. I am shocked and so grateful that this is the ending of the difficult and, at times, unbearable situation I went through all of those years ago. I am so proud that I am doing my best to put something good into the world. I feel lucky that anyone cares what I have to say.

I have already gotten to meet and chat with so many inspiring people. I have been able to tell my story and to share *Listen, Lucy* with complete strangers and gain their support in my mission to create a more accepting world. I have been able to read the most humbling, beautiful and powerful stories of ordinary people dealing with difficult circumstances who are still doing extraordinary things. How could it get any better?

When I speak to different groups about *Listen, Lucy,* I talk about confidence and self-acceptance. I tell them how insecure and down on myself I was for such a long time because of how I am wired and all of the things that were "wrong" with me. I speak about how my anxiety completely controlled me. I talk about how I completely embrace who I am and am fully confident in the person I have become. By saying that, I don't mean that I am happy every day and that things are easy. Anxiety is a constant struggle for me and believing in my dream is a lot easier said than done on certain days. However, right now, I am at a place in my life where I am ready to take the biggest leap of faith I have ever taken.

So, my big announcement:

I have officially put in my notice at my full-time job and am going to pursue *Listen, Lucy* as my career. I cannot believe this is all happening! This is the scariest, coolest, most exciting and terrifying thing I have ever done. #LucyTakesTheWorld—I know it is not the entire world just yet but humor me, okay?

I hope you all continue to follow *Listen, Lucy* and what I am trying to do. Your support is overwhelmingly incredible to me. I can't thank you enough for every kind, thoughtful, inspiring and even sometimes hilarious message I receive from so many of you. This will never get old for me. Ever.

So, here is to hoping! Hoping that people continue to love my message of acceptance. Hoping that I stay confident in pursuit of my dream. Hoping that *Listen, Lucy* positively impacts people's lives. Hoping that the readers and writers of this website learn to accept themselves, flaws and all, and see that we really are in this together. And lastly, here is to hoping that I can tell people who are going through a difficult time what I wish I could tell my younger self:

"Push through it. Stay focused. You are definitely not alone in this. In the end, you are going to do something really cool with all you are going through. Trust yourself."

Jordan

Listen, Lucy -

My life has had its ups and downs. There have been many hardships and struggles, but through it all, I have tried to remain grateful and stay focused on the positives along the way.

I have worked very hard, and consider myself extremely fortunate. I was introduced to Listen, Lucy through a work project for a client. I don't believe in coincidences. Everything happens for a reason. I was touched by the stories, and by the incredible ripple effect of kindness and encouragement that can be generated - just by sharing these stories.

I have always found that you get what you give out of life. And even in the hardest of times, when I had nothing to give, and often relied on the kindness of others to just get by, I still had my smile. No one can take that away... and sometimes the only thing someone else really needs are a few kind words and a smile.

And so the kindness of a handwritten card containing "Pay It Forward" cards have inspired me so far in the following ways - I was driving my son to school this morning and there was a woman whose car had broken down in the middle of the road. She looks pretty upset so I pulled over and offered to help push the car to the side of the road. Well, I'm not exactly car-moving strong, but sure enough, 2 more vehicles pulled over, and a few gentlemen hopped out to help. The ordeal ended in a few strangers, smiling and wishing each other a good day.

I walked back to my car and saw the woman walking back towards me with a child about my son's age carrying a backpack. As it turns out, we live in the same development, our kids are in the same grade, and I was able to give them a lift. It's not like I had to go out of my way. Just made a tiny effort to be kind to a stranger.

Tomorrow, I have requested the day off to give a lift to a friend who is having surgery. Why? Because, why not? :)

I may never be rich in material things, but I am blessed with happiness and health. Making a conscious effort to look for ways to "Pay It Forward" only makes all the good energy shine more brightly around you. Choose each day to see the radiance of positivity going on around you, and reflect that back onto the world.

And so on, and so forth...

Thank you for being an inspiration. I promise to keep passing it on.

Listen, Lucy.

I just wanted to say thank you for this website. It is important for people struggling with a problem, no matter what their problem may be, to have an outlet and a place to record their feelings. Thank you for being so brave and for having the courage to tell your story in the hopes that it may have a positive impact on the lives of others.

So I'm sure my story is slightly different than some of the posts that are on your website. My life is going pretty well at the moment and I consider myself very blessed in many ways. I appear very put-together and confident at all times to my family, friends, and peers but the truth is that I am actually struggling when it comes to being intimate with others. Anyone who knows me will tell you that I appear to be one of the strongest, confident, no-bullshit women that they know but the truth is that I keep getting involved with men who use me and don't treat me the way I should be treated. I keep telling myself that I am worth more than this but I keep going back in hopes of finding someone who will love me and accept me for me. I truly have a heart of gold and would do anything for the ones I love....I just want someone to love me back. I understand that other people are going through things that I could never imagine and that are far worse than my problems, however, I am living proof that you never know what a person is going through. On the outside I'm confident and strong and on the inside I'm falling apart.

Listen, Lucy,

Today was probably my toughest day of teaching so far. There is a theory that when you work with middle-schoolers in any area that they are so energetic and have a hard time paying attention. Apparently whoever made this theory did a phenomenal job with their research because it is spot on (I was probably a main piece of evidence for this theory). On top of that, when you work with the middle schoolers that I work with, ones that are incredibly disadvantaged, have been raped and neglected, it makes it that much more difficult.

Today was just like any other day; some students were driving me insane, others were making me crack up, and some were astonishing me with their amazingness (when you are a teacher its incredible how fast one of your students could make your day). But when I walked out to my car at the end of the day I saw that the windshield wipers were moving and my back window was shattered. Someone tried stealing my car from the school parking lot and ripped out the ignition!

I really thought this was going to ruin my day for a couple seconds. Then my students came running out of school furious about what had happened to my car. Every one of them asked if I was doing okay and if there was anything I needed. All of my teachers and the principals came up to me and gave me hugs and asked if there was anything they could do. I told one that I had officially been initiated and she responded, "That's right! You're not a virgin anymore!" (This made me laugh pretty hard).

Just when I was overwhelmed by support, my best friend left what he was doing and drove 30 minutes to pick me up and bring me home. My brother called 4 times to make sure I was okay. Another student teacher offered me a ride back to campus. My parents have done EVERYTHING to make sure that I am fokay. My girlfriend, unaware of what had happened, made me dinner and had it waiting for me in the fridge. Then when I was at the library, two of my favorite people in the world showed up with a present of sour patch kids, sunflower seeds, and Reese's cups (they know the way to my heart). They said they were going to put toy cars in it but they didn't know if it was too soon lol.

So Lucy there are two ways we can remember this day. There was the one bad event that upset me for about 14 seconds, or there were the 100 acts of paying it forward in response to the bad event of the day which made me feel more loved than ever. Lucy, I think you are getting through to people, because before you existed, this writer never would have seen this day for the good. YOU have made me a better person and my life infinitely better! Thank you!

PS. I bought one of my students a notebook and put a Pay it Forward card in it. She decided to pay it forward by drilling me in the back with a freshly sharpened pencil ten minutes later. Not exactly how I would've paid it forward, but who am I to judge? #theacceptancemovement

Listen, Lucy,

It feels like everyone I trust betrays me, and it's felt like this since ... well, since I learned what the word trust meant. My so-called best friend of eight years went behind my back a week or so ago and dated the boy I fell in love with. The boy I'm still in love with. She decided to date him without even bothering to consult me about it. To see if I was okay with that. She didn't do it. And the worst part is that ... that I didn't even find out from her. I found out from a guy friend of mine who I hardly ever even see anymore. She told him before she told me, her supposed "sister" and "best friend." I ... I can safely say I've never felt more betrayed in my entire life than I did in that moment. I felt so vulnerable. So betrayed. I felt so manipulated. I felt weak. And I had no one to talk to about it. No one. Above everything I was feeling, I felt alone and abandoned.

I wish I could say I got on this website when I felt that way, but I didn't. In hindsight, I kinda wish I had. But instead I turned on my video camera and started to talk and ramble and say everything I had never said aloud before. And, for the first time in a long time, I talked so much and so long about things that hurt me and I started to cry. Not even silent tears running down my face but full-on ugly sobbing. I could barely even form coherent sentences. I couldn't think and I couldn't breathe. Everything I kept bottled up inside for a countless amount of years quite literally broke me. That was also the day I had my first and hopefully my only panic attack. Thinking about how I was betrayed, how it wasn't even the first time.

I cannot count how many people I've lost to betrayal, to sneaking around behind my back while I pretend not to notice. While I remained ignorant. But the loss of my best friend tore me apart from the inside out. I cried for hours, I couldn't even sleep without feeling tears burn in my eyes. Luckily, it had been the weekend so I didn't have to go to school and face the girl I once considered to be my "sister." I knew I wouldn't be able to look at her without breaking down in tears. So, for the entire weekend, I cried like a baby because, in this bittersweet and twisted sense, I lost a part of me.

The moral of this is ... betrayal is always going to be a part of your life. Someone out there is always wanting to use you. Manipulate you. Break you. But ... don't let them do that. Don't let them break you or manipulate you. Don't let them think they've won. Cope. Cry. Record a video. Ramble and prattle and let everything resting on your shoulders slowly be lifted away. Talk to someone you know for sure won't betray you.

Just be strong.

Listen, Lucy,

Love is dynamic. There are ups and downs, but for certain the feeling of love doesn't disappear. The exterior may change, but inside, deep and true is love.

With many faces, love is ever-changing-a sort of shape shifter. Let's say that one day love takes shape in the form of a heated argument ending in tears. How can this be love though? It's when you break apart the emotions on the surface that things become clearer. Beneath the surface is the heart beating with love. It's what makes us apologize, feel guilt and care about another to the fullest extent.

But, love can also take the shape of an afternoon of fun. Let's say that love appears in the form of swinging at the local park-the swings we all know from childhood. Laughing and swinging higher and higher, leaning back and becoming a part of the sky. How can this be love? Love is pure bliss where we can let go and be childish again unafraid of being judged. We break apart the surface level emotions of happiness and laughter and beating below is the heart full of love.

Through ups and downs, twists and turns, love remains.

Listen Lucy,

Sometimes something great comes right up out of nowhere and smacks you right in the face. I am really into this pay it forward thing. It brings me true joy. I think it's the unconditionalness (I think I just created a new word) of the whole thing. It's almost like you get to play Santa.

Where I work, a guy came up to me and said that he thinks there are about 5 or 6 kids that we work with that are pretty unlikely to get any Christmas gifts this year.

I got their names and immediately group messaged my closest support system and asked if they were interested. When I say I got a positive response from all parties within a minute I am not lying. And, this was like 2 or 3 days before Christmas. WOW!

I did not go shopping nor did I buy any gifts; but, I did get to play Santa Claus. This is really cool. You never know what is going to happen. As you might imagine, delivering these presents takes you to some really interesting places. Who would have thought Santa has bigger problems than fitting down the chimney.

I've done this many times in the past and it's different than you might think. Sometimes, I just leave presents at the door. Sometimes I deliver them to family members and wish I had more to give. Sometimes I deliver them and not much is said. Sometimes things go off the charts. But to me it is always really, really, really cool.

This year, on Christmas Eve, my son and I went out. We drove various parts of Allegheny County and made our deposits. Things were going fairly efficiently. It was a good day……it was sunny and warm and he and I were enjoying each other's company. It was a good day about to become great.

We found ourselves in a neighborhood that had seen better times when the steel mills were up and running. We were delivering to a young person named Diamond. I got to know Diamond over the last couple of months and she really inspires me. Not because she has everything together but because she trying to get everything together. Diamond is awesome.

I got out of the car and knocked on her door. I had maybe 5 or 6 presents. When they unexpectedly open the door, there was a room full of people mostly very young. When Diamond saw me, her reaction was priceless. She was appreciative and gracious. An attitude of gratitude personified.

She softly repeated my name several times each time followed by "thank you so much, this is so nice." She gave me a hug that I am not soon to forget. My heart was warmed and my eyes were filled. Special.

Because the weather was so cooperative, I didn't know it at the time, but my son, who was still in the car, heard everything. We just looked at each other and smiled. We knew..yep, we knew!

Typically, that would have been the end of it. It's kind of a private thing and I don't look for any follow up information so we just move forward. But not this time. Yesterday, I was sitting in my office when one of my co-workers came in and wanted to tell me that the thing I did for Diamond was really special.

I started to downplay it. Like I said, to me this stuff is from my private side and I really don't like to expound on it at work. But my co-worker had something to share.

As it turned out, one of those young people that was in Diamond's house was from a different, underprivileged country. She is roughly the same age and size as Diamond and she was staying with Diamond and her family temporarily. Christmas was not of immediate concern.

My co-worker informed me when Diamond got her 5 or 6 gifts, she knew that her friend too, would not be receiving gifts this year.

Diamond gave her friend half of her gifts.

Today was a good day.

I have been working so hard on *Listen, Lucy* for more than a year and a half now. I cannot believe how much it has grown. When I think about the day that I started to post about *Listen, Lucy* and what the site looked like then, I am shocked at the progress I have made. Today was another progressive step.

Speaking to young people about my project is a goal I have had from the very beginning. Using my story and what I have been through to spread some acceptance, positivity and hope in the world is something that has become so important to me. Slowly, I have worked to build my site and my brand to the point that people feel comfortable with my ability to present this project to their students. Today, I spoke to two amazing classrooms about *Listen, Lucy* and #TheAcceptanceMovement. It was awesome.

When I was getting my presentation together and practicing it in my car on the way to-and-from my job, I was having a difficult time actually talking about when I was really sick. This really surprised me. I think that sometimes I talk about it a lot and I know what happened, but I don't really allow myself to think back too much into how sick I was. Talking about it in depth really brought some emotions out of me. Speaking to high school students reminded me of the horrible place I was in at their age and how far I have come. Like I say in my presentation, you should never forget where you came from because it helps you appreciate where you are now and makes you love yourself for how hard you fought through it—regardless of what the trauma or tragedy is that you have endured. Everyone has their own issue to handle and deal with—we should be more understanding of that.

In my presentation, I also talk about acceptance and how important it is. Accepting yourself and accepting others. I talk about how the things that I thought were "wrong" with me have now guided me to create *Listen, Lucy* and that you can make something good to put out in the world after you have been through a really difficult situation. I hope this sunk in with some of them. These young kids have their entire lives ahead of them to accomplish awesome things and I hope that the short time I spent with them today helped them to see that. I feel like I could do this forever and really hope that I get the opportunity to do so.

I am obviously head-over-heels in love with this site, #TheAcceptanceMovement, and everything that *Listen, Lucy* is and has come to stand for in the short time it has been around. Just when I thought I couldn't love it anymore, a young girl came up to me at the end of my presentation and said she wanted to formally introduce herself to me. She seemed nervous as she told me that she loves what I am doing and was so happy I was there today. She told me she hopes she can do what I am doing one day. It was the coolest thing. I just may have helped her out in some way. Even if she is the only person that will ever come up and say that to me for the rest of my life—*Listen, Lucy's* mission has been accomplished.

Today was a really good day.

Jordan

Listen, Lucy,

Up until August 2014, I was in a committed relationship with my first real boyfriend. We were together a total of 4 years, over which I convinced myself that happiness was tacky, overrated and honestly somewhat unattainable. Indeed, I was completely delusional.

We have been apart just a few short months, but during this time I have found the person that lost herself in a relationship that was emotionally draining. My ex was very good to me; he showered me with compliments, gifts, attention and affection. I loved him, but I was not in love with him—something that took me a long time to realize. The relationship was emotionally draining for one reason: he relied entirely on me as his source of happiness. Being that he was a somewhat negative, glass-is-half-empty-kind of guy this was a pretty heavy burden to bear. But I loved him and fought through it to bring him joy when I could. Little did I know that putting all my energy into bringing one single other person happiness took all my time away from making myself happy and nurturing the other relationships in my life. This turned into a vicious cycle because the truth is, you can't make others happy unless you are truly happy. As much as we loved each other, we took each other's happiness away.

For two (long) years we remained in this limbo of unhappiness. This isn't to say I don't have wonderful memories with him. It was like a marathon of unhappiness with a few short spurts of happiness. So why did this last so long? One word: fear. We became each other's security blanket, which is why it was so hard to break away. It was only once I hit rock bottom, once I was so undeniably aware of my unhappiness that I mustered up the courage to break away.

I've never, ever been happier.

I've found this light inside me that was overcast by the relationship for so long. My friendships have improved; my family life has improved, every day I find it harder not to smile. I never knew that this kind of happiness was even possible and I'm so grateful for the life I have. The risk might have felt huge, but the reward was greater than I could have ever imagined.

Listen, Lucy,

The builder lifted his old gray head.

"Good friend, in the path I have come," he said,

"There follows after me today

A youth whose feet must pass this way.

This stream, which has been as naught to me,

To that fair youth may a pitfall be.

He too must cross in the twilight dim —

Good friend, I am building this bridge for him."

I remember when I was about 16 or so, we were helping a friend move. We were in the act of moving something very heavy when my dad gave way a let me and others do the lifting. This was the first time the thought ever occurred to me that my dad was beginning to age.

To me, my dad was a mountain of a man, a pillar of strength, a rock. Was I beginning to see a chink in his impenetrable armor?

Now it's many years later and not just my dad but his whole generation has aged. Many of his closest friends are no longer with us. My mom is no longer with us. I've watched family and friends battle sickness and loneliness; become frail and vulnerable. Sometimes it can be difficult to watch. But, being difficult to watch is not an excuse for not helping.

These very people that have helped me so many times are in need. Am I helping enough?

I miss my mom. I think back to all of the little things that she did for me. How many dinners did she cook for me? How many times did she correct things that I didn't do so well? How many good things did she try and teach me that I didn't listen to? I know she's proud of who I am and what I have become, but there is still a question in my mind if I thanked her enough. Was there more that I could have done?

My father-in law has digressed in recent years. In his younger years and even his mid-life years he was bigger than life. He would help anybody, anytime, anywhere. I was probably the recipient of his help more than anyone. The other day he and I were riding in my car going to get a strawberry milkshakes. We were at a red light when I said to him, "thank you for everything you have done for me". I think he thought I was crazy.

Like many of us, during my younger years I didn't appreciate how good I had it. I took too many things for granted. I really didn't know what was important. My dad and my relationship was fine but it could have been so much better. All that I had to do was make a little effort. Since my mom passed, I have been spending a lot more time with my dad. I think we have learned so much more about each other. Our relationship has become special. I always knew he was a great man but now I know he is great for so many more reasons. I'll never be able to repay him for everything he has done for me.

I, too, am starting to age. I am not able to do some of the things that I used to be able to do. I have been blessed with a great family and friends. Things have turned out well because of the great people that showed me the way. When I look back to all of those that have helped me, for many reasons, I know that it would be impossible to repay them. But, the one thing I thing learned from these influential people, the best way to repay them and others is by paying it forward. I better get busy!

The half marathon was a couple of weeks ago. It was such an exhilarating, difficult, and rewarding experience. I knew I wanted to write about this accomplishment in my life and as I sat down to reflect on what I was going to say, I was surprised in the direction my message went.

I was going to start off by saying that for my entire life I have struggled with body image, but as I seriously thought about the different stages of my life, I realized that wasn't true. Until I was eighteen years old, I played at least three sports a year. I was so active and constantly running, jumping, diving and scrambling that I never really thought about what I consumed and how many calories each meal had or if I was going to gain weight or not. The thought didn't cross my mind at all. I was the size I was and I was happy about it.

Once I stopped playing sports and went to college, got through my illnesses and got healthy, I started to put on weight. I was no longer active and I wasn't that aware of what I was eating or drinking. Like most, I really struggled with body image. At different times in my life, I have been consumed by losing weight, dieting and constantly ripping myself apart mentally for what I have looked like. I ate salsa for lunch (I am not exaggerating) for about a year in preparation for my wedding. I thought about losing weight for my wedding dress just as much, if not more, than I thought about how excited I was to get married. I thought it was normal.

After training and running for a half marathon—I love my body. Not so much for what it looks like but for what it has accomplished.

It has weathered gradual hills, neverending mountains, early mornings, unbearable humidity, not to mention miles and miles and miles. It pushed me a step further when my I had decided it was too difficult to run for one more minute. When my head said it was time to stop, my body reminded me to not give up. There were times that my legs literally felt like cement but they really never let me down. It is actually incredible.

I have to be honest, I lost weight during the training process and that makes me happy as well. But losing the weight wasn't my first priority so it was just like a nice little bonus. I feel like I appreciate and accept my body differently after having put it through the ringer.

My honest hope is that I can continue feeling this positive about myself. That I can remain proud of myself, continue the running and enjoy the pasta I am consuming. I hope I can always love my body for what it has helped me accomplish and not be so damaging to myself because I have never been, and will never be, a size zero. Is this something I can say with full confidence that I will always remember? Of course not. But for now, it is nice to have a little peace in my mind that I am good with who I am and what I look like. It is also nice to be able to confidently share this with you.

We should all strive to be a little nicer to ourselves.

#TheAcceptanceMovement

Jordan

Listen, Lucy

I trust my heart and hex the ground

with hopes of love to lift me abound

I thatch the stone and throw it swift

I respect my tears and off I lift

towards the light

towards the dark

took strange to change and made the spark

ignite your past to extinguish its stay

embrace your fire

for its now

today...

Listen, Lucy:

I am a freshman in college. I have been in relationship before. My most serious relationship was my sophomore year of high school it was the first guy I truly loved and said it too. By the end he was abusive with his words and I would take it. He kept me on a leash and I let him. I lost a lot of friends, connections, and missed a lot of events. He broke up with me leaving me heartbroken I was crushed and he knew I was so even after we broke up he was still able to drag me along thinking he still loves me. I finally figured him out and stopped it. However my junior, senior year I was used by four guys sexually (not all at the same) and at the time I thought that meant he liked me and we would date soon, but then they would leave me for a pretty, more better girl. I was crushed every single time I would cry myself asleep. This past summer I finally was in a real relationship (or so I thought). He seemed caring and different to me but a week before I left for college he dumped me said all he wanted was a summer fling didn't even have feelings for me. I have never felt that heartbroken since my sophomore year. I don't have feelings for him anymore because he crushed mine. But it did scar me and made me give up. I feel like I will never find the right guy for me he isn't out there. I have been hurt too much that my guard is a steel wall that is 10 feet thick. I am tired of the tears. On top of that I won't get to have the family I have always wanted. Most important I feel like I will never have that person who is my world who knows how to treat me in any situation. Bringing tears to my eyes. I am done and I give up on trying to have that person...

Listen, Lucy:

I know you've lost someone and it hurts. You may have lost them suddenly, unexpectedly. Or perhaps you began losing pieces of them until one day, there was nothing left. You may have known them all your life or you may have barely known them at all. Either way, it is irrelevant – you cannot control the depth of a wound another soul inflicts upon you.

Which is why I am not here to tell you tomorrow is another day. That the sun will go on shining. Or there are plenty of fish in the sea. What I will tell you is this; it's okay to be hurting as much as you are. What you are feeling is not only completely valid but necessary -- because it makes you much more human. And though I can't promise it will get better any time soon, I can tell you that it will – eventually. For now, all you can do is take your time. Take all the time you need." –Lang Leav

I do not necessarily have all of the right words to describe how I am feeling through my heartbreak, but after reading this quote I have become more hopeful. I am hopeful to love again, and not love someone or something but to love my life. I have realized that I do not have to have it all figured out to move forward, just as long as I don't turn around. Heartbreak isn't easy and hearts don't heal in a day but when they do they love better than ever and I cannot wait till then.

Listen, Lucy,

Time is the only resource that can never be restored once it is gone... Yesterday can never be pulled forward, because we have lost yesterday, which makes today infinitely precious".

I will be the first to admit that I don't take full advantage of the gift of time; I really don't think anyone does, it's impossible. But the time that I am thinking about isn't time to get work done to get ahead in your professional life or something of that nature. I'm talking about the time we spend with people--- friends, loved ones, or anyone who puts a smile on our face.

When I think about not taking full advantage of the time God has granted me it puts a knot in my stomach. Especially the time wasted fighting with people we care deeply about or simply not enjoying or appreciating the time that we get to spend with them. I had a very special person in my life lose a battle to cancer; everyone knows that terrible feeling. I listen to her voicemail saved on my phone all the time; I would do anything for one more minute to see her smile or to hear her laugh.

But on a less tragic note, within the past year I became very close with someone who really changed my outlook on life. He would sit down and talk to me, give me advice and books to read. I wrote down all of his sayings and put them on a poster board in my room so I could pass them along to someone who might need those wise words just like I did. A couple of months ago he texted me and told me he needed to see me immediately---he got a new job and would be moving that night—although we still remain in contact, that time together will never be the same again. Just like that, he was gone.

We all know the saying that time doesn't wait for anybody, well it's the truth. Everyday truly is a gift that we will never be able to return. Our challenge isn't just to make the most of that time, it's to appreciate and enjoy that time that is given to us with the people we are privileged enough to share it with because they will not be there forever.

Recently I was able to spend a lot of time with my Godfather, just me and him. I don't get to do that too often. We laughed a lot and made memories that both he and I won't ever forget. I soaked in every ounce of happiness I felt just to be able to hang out with him for a couple of hours. Every day that I drove to meet him I took a minute to slow down and realize how special this time truly was. For the first time in a long time I wasn't taking the greatest gift of all for granted.

I'm currently in my last football season that I will ever play, and with every end of practice more sadness creeps in. Today is our first game and I can't sleep for one more second. I'm sitting here thinking about how special this has all been, about all the memories that I have made. My family has come to every single game that I have ever played in, and trust me they have traveled great lengths to do so. The friends that I have made will be ones that last forever. In fact, one of my best friends in the world will be coaching against me on the other sideline, talk about weird. But as I sit here and write this, I play the voicemail from my grandma and my eyes instantly fill with tears. I would give absolutely anything to see her in the stands today, I know she would love it. Of all the lessons she taught me, how to love, laugh, and care for others, the one she is teaching me right now is the one I need most.

Don't ever take time for granted; cherish it, and enjoy it while it's there. If I can do that, I know at the end of all this I'll be able to look back on my life with a smile on my face.

When I sat down to write this entry, I wasn't quite sure how to get out what I wanted to say. I knew the story that I wanted to tell, but I wasn't quite sure how to form the message and to do the experience justice. A lot of times when I am feeling anxious, my thoughts get jumbled. It is hard for me to focus and my heart starts racing. That being said, I am going to do my best.

My grandma passed away almost two years ago. She died of bone cancer and it was a really difficult thing to watch happen to someone who had been so full of life and laughter. It was painful and is something I think about often. Working for an organization that is trying to find a cure for blood cancer, I often think about those who have experienced losses like mine—some of cancer's victims being so much younger than my grandma. It is something that weighs heavy on me.

My dad and I have decided to run a half marathon and raise funds for the Leukemia and Lymphoma Society. We have raised over five thousand dollars. It is something that I am so incredibly proud of and a time I will remember forever. The training is hard. It is physically draining and mentally exhausting.

Some of you know this story I am about to tell.

On one particular run, I was struggling. My dad and I were running eight miles and we were only two in. My dad has often talked about the Blue Heron he saw out in the lake many moons ago and how it gives him a peaceful, easy feeling. He told me he wished I would be able to see it one day.

As we were running along the lake, my dad yelled to me, "Jord!" I panicked, thinking someone was about to hit me with their car. Once I realized I was safe, my dad pointed out the Blue Heron to me. He had a lot of emotion in his eyes as he told me about the night before. He had said a small prayer to my grandma, his mom, to let us see the Blue Heron on our run the next day. As I stared at the bird, I said to my dad, "I wish I could see him fly."

We started running again, this time with a conversation that was focused on my grandma and her final days. We talked about our final words to her and how our entire family had sat around her for three days straight before she passed—something that would make her so happy. As we rounded the bend, there was the Blue Heron again—sitting out so we could see him perfectly. Just as my dad called my name to look over, it took off, spreading its wings for me to see. At that moment, I was sure that she was there and that she was proud.

Now, I have no idea what is waiting for us on the other side of this life, but I know for the first time, in a very long time, I felt my grandma's presence. It was a feeling that I will never forget. The Blue Heron has been around every single time my dad and I have run the lake since that day. Every time we see it, it makes us smile. It reminds us of someone who was, and always will be, one of the most important people in our lives. Someone who taught us so much and helped form our morals and values. Someone that we are remembering as we take on this half marathon. GramZ.

Losing someone is always difficult. Every once in a while we are lucky enough to feel like that person is near again. If you find something that gives you that peaceful, easy feeling—hold on tight.

Jordan

Listen, Lucy.

My life up until this point has been a series of decisions that were all based on a vision I had for my life at that particular time. Call me a dreamer, but I've always tried to follow what makes my heart happy, without giving real consideration to what all that may entail.

Today I'm living a life that is a completely skewed, disarrayed portrait of the life I painted for myself as a young girl, a teen, and an optimistic college student. Color me a typical millennial, but 6 months out of college I feel as lost and confused as I was freshmen year. All of my loved ones tell me it's normal to not have it all figured out and it was acceptable for me to make the decisions I made at the time I made them because truthfully: that's what felt right back then.

But it still hurts.

Nobody prepares you for the day-in and day-out that is working 9-5 PM. The routine that forces you into a monotony where days seem to slip by faster than the next and all that you've managed to accomplish was avoiding eating a cookie from the break table and getting in a workout before bed.

I wish I could be like the twenty-somethings of my generation on Instagram (so many of which are close friends) who pick up and move and create experiences for themselves that they'll remember for the rest of their life. Those people taking the world by storm because staying at home isn't the cool thing to do. I don't know why I feel stuck in this place that is the only place I've known, but I do, and I wish I could stop hating myself for it.

There are so many things I love about my life that I try to tell myself are the reasons I should be happy, but I still don't feel satisfied. But do we ever? I wonder if anyone else is confused. But according to the Facebook and Twitter versions of all of my friends--everyone else is having the time of their lives.

Today I'm realizing that I chased another phantom reality with the career path I was convinced was the right one and now, it seems, I'm back at square one. I also struggle with knowing how blessed I've been in my life. So then I feel guilty for wanting more. It's turned into a downward and spiraling process of trying to figure out who I am while also trying not to dislike that person at the same time. Now, I have so many things to consider in deciding what my next move should be and some days it seems like it may never be okay. I guess my biggest fear in all of this is that I'll let this battle with myself and my fear of taking risks hold me back from experiencing all it is that I want to experience in life.

The more I grow the more I realize so much can be learned from experiences and sharing them with others. On days like this, I wish someone would tell me they feel the same way. Or even better, I wish someone could say "hey, I've been there, and it all turns out alright." So I hope that by sharing here, someone who's feeling lost, confused, and without a sense of direction, knows that someone else gets it, too.

Sincerely,

Typical (?) Twenty-Something

Listen Lucy,

I used to think I was special. Special because every once in a while when I got into a critical situation God would talk directly to me. It wasn't like I saw a burning bush or heard a loud voice or anything like that. A thought would just pop into my brain that I knew came from God. I knew right when the thought popped into my brain that if I did it, the outcome was going to be good. I felt special because while I do believe, I really wouldn't consider myself overly religious. Why would God be doing this for me?

When I was younger, I was misguided. It was a voluntary choice. I made a conscious effort to be rebellious, uncooperative and intentionally out of control. I wanted that reputation -- reckless abandon. There are consequences with that. Hurt relationships and burned bridges, two DUI's and 3 totaled cars. The outcome probably deserved to be fatal or worse. I could have gotten hurt or killed others. At the time I knew this was a possibility but, I didn't care. It was about me. When I look back on this now, I feel that I am on borrowed time. I feel I have a responsibility to do better for others because it was God's will to see me through these destructive times.

My life was chaotic, but in all of that chaos, a clear message entered my brain – enlist in the service. Little did I know at the time that this decision would prove to serve as the foundation for my life. The benefits would come later. I served three fairly successful years and ended my enlistment with an honorable discharge. My recklessness improved somewhat but the progress was relatively short-lived. Once returning home to my old neighborhood, I looked to get back to my old reputation – recklessness.

Two more totaled vehicles, blown employment opportunities, surely a disaster was looming. In the midst of all of this chaos, a beautiful princess entered my life and showed interest in me. A voiced popped into my brain, marry this girl. Although unlikely at the time, through a miracle, it happened. I married a beautiful woman and a short time later we were blessed with our first child. I can remember being alone in the hospital with my new born and holding her in my arms when the most positive feeling of responsibility popped into my brain. I have to say from that minute forward everything changed for the better.

I got a new entry level job with a local company. Thanks to my veteran status, I was able to pursue a formal education. It seemed that the promotions I received coincided with the degrees that I earned. My family life and career skyrocketed. This improved status was sustained for a number of years but there was still something, something that was drawing me in to that voluntary state of recklessness. It was there hiding in plain sight. It was the alcohol. That's when the thought popped in my head … stop drinking.

I am in my 8th year of sobriety and I know it sounds lame but I never knew life could be this good. My beautiful wife and I are blessed. We have witnessed some of the most precious things parents can ever ask for – college graduations and weddings just to name a few. Grandchildren are right around the corner.

With age comes wisdom. I used to think I was special. I used to think God talked to me directly now and again. Now I know, God was always talking to me. Those times…that the thoughts were popping into my head… those were the times that I was listening.

Listen, Lucy...

Losing control can be terrifying.

For me, it started with tests. Tons of tests by tons of doctors who couldn't give me any answers. There was something obviously wrong but no one could tell me what it was. The diseases the doctors were suggesting were life-changing, maybe even life-ending. I was pricked and poked and observed. Thrown from room to room. No one could figure out why I was struggling so much.

I was losing a lot of weight and looking lifeless. Rumors started to swirl around the hallways as to what was really going on. I couldn't control anything. The anguish of not having any answers is something I wouldn't wish on my worst enemy.

The tests continued. The not- knowing continued. I was losing sleep and I was losing the energy for life that I once had.

I was put on so many different medicines I can't even begin to figure out what they were or how many there were. However, I can tell you that the side effects from these different medications were unbearable. I needed to get control. I had been struggling for over a year and there were no answers. I was sick of everyone asking me what was wrong so I lied every day.

When I started to put some weight back on, I started to down spiral. I was completely out of control, but completely in control if that makes any sense. My mind changed. I couldn't control the doctors or the symptoms I was having, but I could control what went into my body and what I forced out of my body. I began to make myself throw up.

For a long time, I thought this was about the way I looked. I thought I was obsessed with being afraid to gain weight. That was never what it was about. I can see that now. It was about having control over something when I had control over nothing for so long.

I was in so deep I couldn't get out. It was the lowest time in my life. I am still in disbelief that I allowed myself to get taken over like that. I am shocked about how it made sense in my mind.

Through years of counseling I was able to see what I went through and how it got me to that place. It has been many years since I was that lost person. I am much stronger now. I am also really open about my life, but not this.

We all have parts of our past we would rather not admit. Secrets that we keep locked up so the world can't see them. I think that is okay. I think you should share what you are comfortable with, but I also know that I will never forget that dark place I was in. I am not sure if I will ever come to terms with it.

Writing this anonymously has been uplifting for me. Admitting what happened without revealing who I am is just what I needed. Acknowledging this part of my life was needed. I may not want my face plastered next to this story, but it is good to get it out. As strange as it sounds, I never want to forget that part of my life. You can't appreciate how far you have come and who you have become if you don't know where you have been.

To anyone out there struggling like I have: Keep pushing through the darkness. Keep climbing out of the hole. You will find yourself. Don't ever, ever, ever give up on yourself. Giving up is not an option. You will get through it. Your darkness is overwhelming now, I am sure. But the light? The light after the darkness is the most beautiful thing in the world.

I have had many phases in my life. I have never had a hard time moving on from one phase to the next. Leaving high school to go to college was the best day of my life. Leaving college for the real world was really sad and a bit scary, but I was ready. Moving out of my parents' house to my first apartment was exciting. Buying my first home and getting married was all I had ever dreamed of and more. I have never had a hard time accepting moving on and I look back at most of the stages of my life fondly. However, there was one part of my life that always made me feel a knot in my stomach.

I played sports for fourteen years. It consumed my life. It was all I cared about. When I stepped on the court or out into the field, I turned into a different person. I sacrificed my health and my sanity in order to stay on the court for one more second, for one more game. My athletic career ended bitterly as I was having unexplained health issues that I couldn't get under control. It took a toll on me physically for sure, but what it did to me mentally was something I can't explain. After an unbearable basketball season in my senior year of high school, I quit track that upcoming spring. I remember crying while walking down the hall after leaving my coach's office. I remember thinking that my life was over. How silly.

I swore off sports for the next eight years. It was no longer a part of me. I always tell people that, in the end, my body physically rejected me being an athlete so I had no choice but to stop caring about it. I joke that the last day I walked out of the gym at North Hills High School was the last day I ever shot a basketball. I continued to work out but stopped taking it seriously. I stopped running myself into the ground. I realized it wasn't healthy for me and I moved on and never looked back. In my mind, sports brought nothing to the table for me anymore. It was a part of my past and that was all it would ever be. It was a part of my life I would try to push away from me—until recently.

I have started to train for a half marathon that I will be running at the end of October. My dad and I are running together and raising money for the Leukemia and Lymphoma Society. I haven't challenged myself like this in almost a decade. I was really worried and was really dreading the training—until I got out there and started to run the miles. I forgot how therapeutic training is. I forgot what it was like to push myself further than I thought was possible. I forgot how much I thrived when accomplishing something I didn't think I could do. I forgot why I loved it so much.

I am not entirely sure what my message is with this post. It is just a revelation I had when I was running this past weekend. Maybe I finally feel at peace with a phase of my life that ended unfortunately. Maybe I feel like this is the realization that I have my health, and how lucky I am to have it. Maybe it brought back the good memories I had about something that used to define me. Who knows.

I know being an athlete taught me how to compete, work hard, and to be a team player. It taught me leadership and perseverance. It showed me how strong of a person I am. All of these things have helped form me into the adult I am today. The things that led me to be captain of my basketball and soccer teams may also be the very things that helped me land my new job. I guess you never know how one phase of your life will connect you to the next.

I feel grateful for my experience today and I feel happy to share them with you. I am looking forward to seeing what other revelations I have while on my long runs on Saturdays. I will keep you posted.

Jordan

Listen, Lucy:

I am trapped inside a bottle of my own emotions and frustrations. I have been told in the past to 'let things go' or 'brush it off' and yet the emotions remain. I hold things in. They dwell in my mind like an unwanted guest, reminding me every morning that they are still there. My days consist of internal debates about what to do with these feelings, but nothing is ever resolved. I am trapped inside of a bottle that is almost full, a bottle that is about to burst into a million glass pieces.

When I lay down at night my thoughts race, replaying everything that is bothering me. I know letting things out would make me and the people around me feel better, but doing so is not always so easy. I retreat to quiet and secluded places to let my thoughts and feelings rest, thinking I am doing the right thing, yet the thoughts weigh me down like a ton of bricks.

I realize now after 21 years that this has been a problem my entire life, leaving me empty yet full at the same time. I have come to a conclusion that changes need to be made if I want to be the happiest person I can be. I have a select few people in my life that know how severe this problem is for me and have helped me along the way. They have made suggestions of how to deal with this silent struggle, now it is just up to me to make the change.

Since April, I have made changes to let things out that bother me and let things go that cannot be changed. I have had a lot of support and still tend to struggle but it has gotten better and will continue to get better as I open up and release the feelings that weigh me down.

Listen, Lucy-

Over the last few months, I have come across meaningful quotes and Bible verses. Others have been sent my way to remind me of my worth and to remind me of how many people I have in my corner that I mean the world to. This is for you guys and girls. My family. My friends. My rocks. My entire world. I thank you and I appreciate you, each and every moment of my life.

I often visit this Bible verse when I am feeling down. My dear friend shared it with me. She's the best. It reads: "the pain that you've been feeling can't compare to the joy that's coming." Romans 8:18. It reminds me that this too shall pass, that the sun will rise tomorrow, and that I will find love again...

He said he didn't love me anymore. I didn't believe it then, I don't believe it now. You can't just be with someone for three years and drop them like they are last years hot fashion trend. It doesn't make sense. I don't know that it ever will. We had so many great times together. He made me laugh. He made me feel beautiful. But none of this matters to me anymore, because I do know this...

I am the strongest I have ever been. I am the happiest I have ever been. I deserve so much more than whatever that was. Sure I have my days of sadness, but my days of love and laughter far exceed my days of sadness. I have reconnected with old friends, I have spent much more time with the people that really matter to me, and I could not be more appreciative to have had this chance to reassess what really matters in my life. I finally woke up. This was an epiphany that I needed.

I have learned who I am and that who I am right now is who I want to be. I have gained confidence in many different aspects of my life. For instance, I do not particularly enjoy traveling alone. Recently, I ran though the airport, by myself, and made it to the gate just in time to board the plane. I did it. I know this may sound silly, but it was liberating. I don't need someone to complete me. I complete me. Sure, it would be nice to find the man of my dreams and I know in time, I will. But right now, I am working on me. I am working on living my life to the fullest. I am working on being the best person that I can be. I am not going to settle for someone who does not appreciate me. For someone who doesn't notice and value the amazing and unique woman that I am.

I'm sure you have had heart break in your life. But take it from a girl who thought she knew what she wanted. Take it from this girl who thought she knew who and what made her happy. God works in mysterious ways. Everything happens for a reason. It may not make sense when it happens, but it will some day. Remember this...

"Sometimes the bad things that happen in our lives put us directly on the path to the best things that will ever happen to us." Always have faith. Don't waste days being sad over people who are not worth it. We only have so much time on this Earth. Choose to be happy. Choose to make a difference. Choose to accept the love that is most definitely all around you.

The awesome thing about being open about your struggles is that there are times when things come full circle. You remember talking about how bad it was at a certain point in your life and you realize that maybe, in that time, that you got a grip on your situation. For me, there are a couple of different times when I look back and I think, "That's when I got it."

One of those times was when I discovered *Post Secret*, the books by Frank Warren. When my brother took me to Borders and sat me down and showed me this series, something changed with me. I finally saw that people everywhere are dealing with their own nightmares and I am not alone in this. Not at all. I remember my brother reading through one of the books and showing me one certain post card. It was a beautiful pink flower with, "My anxiety controls me," written on it. Even writing about it now makes me tear up because I remember feeling so desperate to feel normal and for someone to understand me. Even though it was anonymous and whoever wrote it will never know how much it meant to me—I felt connected to someone for the first time.

Another a-ha moment happened while I was studying abroad in London. It was my first trip alone. I had gone to high school and college with my friends and my boyfriend and I very rarely went to the store without someone I knew, let alone another country. I remember the nerves as I got off the plane and thought, "Okay, now what?" If I had a panic attack, if my anxiety controlled me while I was there, not only would it ruin my entire experience, but no one was there to help me. It forced me to stop relying on other people to drop everything and be by my side. It forced me to get from point A to point B without having a meltdown. Being in unknown territory was always something that made me uncomfortable but, once I got to London, I saw that not only could I manage to do it, but that I was enjoying every minute of every day. There are so many examples of different things that happened on my trip there that made me feel like it was the happiest and healthiest I have ever been. London launched me into finally becoming healthy again. Deciding to take the risk to go there may be one of the most important decisions of my life.

Lastly, this website has brought me the biggest understanding of what I have been through, who I have become, and where I want to go. When I came up with this idea, I just wanted to find a way to help people. When I launched the site a year ago, I had never been so excited or nervous in my life. I was literally about to tell everyone I knew about my struggle in the hopes of helping others see that, while we all may not understand exactly what you are going through, we all have our own personal trauma we are dealing with. I felt so happy to be putting this out into the world but I didn't realize how much it was going to continue to help me. It has made me understand people. It has made me see that people I know are fighting through things that I didn't even know about. I have learned just how strong and resilient people are and I have seen that the people who write in and follow this site, work through their problems and come out on the other side with a strong, positive outlook that cannot be taken away. I learn more from this site and it helps me more than I could have ever imagined.

With having a year of *Listen, Lucy* under my belt, I feel like I am not sure what is to come of it. I am excited for the future and want to continue to help others express what is going on and I want this site to help create a better world—one with less judgment and more understanding.

I have learned that while my daily panic attacks are long gone, I continue to struggle from time to time and that's when I turn to this site for inspiration and for a reality check. It calms me. It grounds me and it definitely humbles me. Thank you for being there for my first year of pursuing a dream of mine and for helping me show this small part of the world that we are all in this together.

Cheers to one year and to fifty more!

Jordan

Listen, Lucy:

To Mr. Misleading,

When I look back at when we first met, I don't remember you the way that I do now. I don't remember you affecting my every day; my personality, my behaviors, my overall poor choices. It was innocent then, you didn't control me. I'm not quite sure when that changed. I guess I can look back and see signs that you would eventually overtake me, but none so powerful that I could predict my feelings about you today. Many years after our first meeting, you became more important to me than I ever wanted you to become. I didn't ask for your presence to be so overwhelming, although you had a different plan for your part in my life. You became the thing I turned to, the one constant in what seemed to be an unfair life in my eyes. Too much pressure, too many expectations, too many things that should have happened that didn't. And you numbed all of them. Through thick and thin, you were there. Some good times sure, but mostly you created a chain of events that eventually would spiral out of control. I'm not sure where I lost hold of your power of me, but all I need to know at this point in my life, is that you won that battle at that time. The thing I hate the most about you is that yes, I didn't ask for you to overtake me. But more importantly, that I saw signs and still continued to allow you to be most important in my life. Every day you reared your ugly head. I would try my hardest to run away as fast as I could, but you were faster and stronger than I ever was. I used to pride myself on being strong, on knowing right from wrong, on knowing when enough was enough. But with you, it was different. You ran me until I almost died. And that wasn't good enough. You still hadn't killed me, and your plan was to not stop until you did. I know this now. I know your game, and I know your plan. Good news for me is that I did finally get it. I am finally faster and stronger than you ever thought I could be. Bad news for you is that I'm done. I'm done with the vicious cycle of dealing with you. Dealing with the façade you created when all the while you were just killing me inside. Dealing with the numbness you caused for a moments time, only for reality to eventually set back in. I did it for too long, and I'm tired. It's safe to say that you'll always linger around, waiting for me to come back, plotting your grand plan that you haven't yet completed. I've accepted that. I can tell you today that you can keep waiting, because I'm not coming back. I'm happy. I'm free. I finally feel hope. You have no idea how that feels when you caused me to have none for as long as I can remember. So this is goodbye. Goodbye to our tumultuous relationship that I try my hardest to not resent. And I say that because I don't want to live with regret, live in the past of wishing and wanting to do things over. I am who I am today, scars and all, and that's okay with me. I bet you didn't think I'd ever say that, did you? So I choose to not look back and reminisce on how we first met, on how it got to this point. I know you now, and that's all I need to know.

Listen, Lucy:

I've been thinking a lot about my happiness lately. I've been thinking that it seems like something so simple, making yourself happy. But it's actually really complicated. Happiness is one of the first emotions we learn, it's a word we use everyday, probably multiple times a day, to express how we are feeling. Our lives revolve around our happiness – or lack thereof – and I think that's what makes it complicated.

What makes a person happy? That's a question that usually comes with a quick answer; it can be anything, really. A person, a pet, a thought, a purchase, an event. So how do we make ourselves happy? … This question takes a little more thought for me. So say you finally think of what it is that you can do to make yourself happy, and you do it. And then, you're still not happy. It's frustrating. Is it because we always want more? I think we feel unfulfilled sometimes because we're always waiting for the next step. Are we ever really happy in the moment? Or is anticipating the future what gives us happiness? It's a concept that I constantly wrestle with. I realize that we, like our happiness, are constantly evolving. I'm sure I've changed some over the years, but how did the happiest relationship I've ever been in suddenly turn into something that made me completely unhappy? Did I change that much? Did my happiness change that much? Or did I just want more? My whole life, it's always been important for me to strive for more, to do better and constantly improve myself. But I'm learning that at some point, you have to find the balance between the two extremes so you can begin to feel that comfort and fulfillment. And I'm learning that it is not an easy balance to find.

I've been thinking about how I can find peace with my happiness before I drive myself completely crazy with this cyclical thinking. I so badly want to just feel comfortable with my life, where it is and where it's going. I think I'm getting there. It's a little lonely sometimes, but I think doing it on my own is helping. Something I've realized is that I never want to have to depend on someone else for my happiness – that should be up to me. So for now, I need to remind myself daily that I need to enjoy the ride. If another relationship should come my way, I hope that I'm able to enjoy the moments as they come, rather than always waiting for what's next. When I ask myself, "What makes you happy?" I want to be the answer.

It's like the John Lennon quote that every girl had in her AIM profile in high school (yes, I'm guilty as well):

"When I was five years old, my mother always told me that happiness was the key to life. When I went to school, they asked me what I wanted to be when I grew up. I wrote down 'happy'. They told me I didn't understand the assignment, and I told them they didn't understand life."

I'd like to thank John Lennon and his mom for this little piece of inspiration that I have hanging at my desk to this day. And I'd also like to thank Lucy. We are lucky to have you.

Listen, Lucy,

YOUR beauty is more than skin deep.

Sometimes, I hate the way I look naked. "Maybe if my arms and waist were thinner, or maybe if I could just get rid of my inner thighs." That's what I tell myself in the mirror some days. I often wonder if I'll wake up one morning and think differently. Probably not. I'll probably look this way forever. Maybe if I step on the scale and I am 5 lbs lighter, I'll be happier. As if this magic number is an automatic gateway to ultimate happiness. It has to be, because it's the only thing that keeps me from being happy. Everything else in my life is perfect.

The reality is, that's not true. Those things that I used to tell myself every day were false perceptions of my own reality. I recognized that. It wasn't too late for me, fortunately. Even when I was staring at myself in the mirror (all those times), waiting for the pounds to disappear before my eyes, I knew it was irrational. I knew that as I looked at myself, there was a discrepancy between what everyone always told me and how I felt. They would say, "you're beautiful", and I'd say "thank you", but in my head I would think, you must be lying. For some reason, I couldn't look past the skin. These fleeting moments pop up every now and again to haunt me, regardless of how beautiful I know that I am now. When they arise in my head, that's the very moment I have to take a breath and look in the mirror to tell myself, "you're beautiful". It's a constant battle to remind myself that I am me, there is not another like me and there will not ever be another like me. And--and, and, and--I am perfect the way

I am. I love myself.

I have realized that this life is perfect, regardless of how messy and often destructive it can feel. The strength that we build to over come the messiness is what keeps us going every day. My hope for you, and for myself, is to be the best possible version of myself every day and to never stop improving that version of myself. To wake up every morning and be the first person to tell myself, "you are beautiful" and to go out into the world with courage and confidence. If I can be true to myself, I can be true to others. As they say, you can't do it alone.

Listen, Lucy,

The moment that you find out that you are going to be a parent is one of the most crazy, exciting moments in your life…We were ready. Ready for the pregnancy. Ready for the changes. Ready for the joy. Ready to be a Mom and Dad.

Just as quickly as joy can fill your life, horror can consume it.

For all the parents out there who have had a miscarriage, our hearts go out to you. For all the would be mothers that have had to attend baby showers or witness their friends and family have children while putting aside your own personal terror. We pray for you.

We didn't think it was ever going to happen. Two years and three miscarriages has a way of making a couple lose faith. The kind words, "it's going to happen for you two" and "just keep trying" did little to restore that faith that was stolen from us.

Throughout this disaster, we found each other. We consoled each other. After a terrible experience with a doctor, we were blessed to have found the most amazing doctor to have ever taken a breath on this earth. She listened. She let frustration and tears pour out so patiently before she offered her expertise. She restored faith.

14 short weeks ago we found out we were pregnant! All is well and the baby is progressing beautifully. As each day passes, we are one day closer to meeting our little bundle. But we will never forget the past.

This is our success story. Many of you have similar ones. Some may not have found your success yet. Find Hope.

Listen, Lucy,

I've always been a confident person. Anyone who knows me knows that I over prepare for everything that I do, that I am an extremely hard worker. Because I am always over prepared I rarely ever get nervous or scared, but what happens when I face a situation that I am not prepared for?

The other night I was lying in bed unable to sleep. I'm almost done with my junior year of college, which means I am going to be in the real world soon. I'm going to be teaching America's youth in less than two years. That's when I realized I have no f***ing clue what I am doing. Are you kidding me? I'm going to be 22 years old and responsible for the growth and development of so many young students? I started sweating and for the first time in a long time I doubted myself.

I think one of my main problems is that I always expect perfection out of myself. This isn't a bad thing, it's actually a great thing. It's made me who I am today. I've never been the type of person who just gets things right away; I've always envied those people though. My imperfections have driven me to work harder, over prepare, and physically/mentally will myself to success.

Just like everything else, I expect to be the perfect teacher when I walk into my first classroom. Guess what my man? That's impossible!!! I realized why I feel like I have no idea what I am doing. It's because I don't! But that's more than okay, because that doesn't mean that I'm not going to be a good teacher. In fact, I think I'm going to be an amazing teacher. I just have to take it slow, and realize that I can only learn from experience, not from some text book.

I guess that's my message that I want to share with everyone. Don't be nervous or scared about something in your life because you don't know what you're doing. No one knows what they are doing until they go out there and do it. You are going to fail, you should! Don't let it deter you from your dreams or shake your confidence. Rather let it motivate you and learn from it. I read something on this site once that I have since always tried to keep in mind, "Slow down, get in the right hand lane and go the speed limit." I'm not going to be the best teacher in the world the first day I walk in. Is that still my goal? Of course. Will I fail? Without a doubt. But it's not about doing it right the first time, only on the rarest of occasions does that occur. It's about having the courage to change the world, the charisma to captivate people's minds, the strength to keep going even when you fail. Slow down and go the speed limit. Don't be scared, be confident in yourself. Don't worry about the results right away, worry about the process itself. If you do that you don't have any reason not to be confident.

I have had a lot of time to reflect on *Listen, Lucy* and all of the incredible submissions I have received so far. I am in total awe of the brave people who have shared their stories and the support I have received from friends, family and complete strangers for telling mine. I have been wanting to post but have not been able to find the words I have been looking for in order to properly get my message out there. I think I have found them now.

I have read through the entire *Listen, Lucy* blog again and have been brought to tears over the struggles so many are facing. I know that feeling in the pit of your stomach where you feel like you can't figure out which way to move. I have seen a lot of different themes throughout the different entries—pain, heartbreak, losing yourself, admitting your flaws and, eventually, success. Through all of the different stories I have read, I have found one common thread that has led to these people getting to the light at the end of their tunnel—their support system.

In a majority of these stories, people have thanked their friends, families, classmates, peers and coworkers for being this rock of support that they couldn't have triumphed without. It has really got me thinking about how important it is to surround yourself with really good people.

I know I talk about my dad a lot and the different things he has told me throughout my life, but while I always knew he was a smart guy, I didn't know how much his words have impacted me until I started writing again. He has always told me that it's okay to make mistakes because everyone does. Big mistakes, small mistakes—they are all inevitable. But there are a few decisions that you have to get right. One of those decisions is the company you keep.

Tough times in your life cause you to question yourself—your strength, your character, and the path you are going down. Your friends, family and significant other should lift you up when you are down. They should show you support and love and care. They should make you laugh. Take a look around at the people you keep close to you. How do they make you feel about yourself? How do they feel about themselves? Do they enrich your life or weigh you down?

I want to thank my support system—my incredible family who has always been there for me. My hilarious and unbelievably supportive friends who believe in me more than I could ever believe in myself and my brand new husband—who is not brand new to my life—you have always been the greatest partner. When it comes to the company I keep in my life, I like to think that I nailed it.

I want to leave you with a quote I came across.

"You become like the five people you spend the most time with. Choose wisely."

Jordan

Listen, Lucy,

For the last 3 months or so i have been...lost. i am not me, and i do not know who i am supposed to be anymore. i cannot find myself; i'm just am here, floating along.

i am letting something take over my life and impact me entirely. it's something that doesn't deserve to have this power over me. i'm caught tossing and turning at night, stress weighing on my mind, worry, fear, panic. i wake up with a knot in my stomach; there aren't enough hours. i don't sleep, i'm not eating right, i'm not taking time for myself. i get home exhausted so i don't want to move; i used to enjoy jogging. i can't concentrate. i don't know where to begin to gain control of my life back, so i just don't. i sit, i stare off, i watch mindless television as my means of escape instead of taking care of myself, my home, my relationship.

my relationship is flatlining. my significant other is becoming nothing more than a roommate - i've been here before and i didn't fix it last time so what makes me feel like i'll be able to this time? i don't know how to fix it. i always push the most important people away without trying, but at the same time, i give up on trying to make things better. why do i get to this place where i feel like it's unfixable and there's no point? shouldn't there be a point? i'm afraid i don't see it anymore.

maybe i am just meant to be alone.

really, all of my relationships are suffering. i've had down times - really, really down times. i've been sad, and i've kept to myself, and i've tried to disappear from the world, but it's never been like this. now i'm annoyed by the people i used to call my best friends. i'm not understanding anybody anymore. i question why people do or don't do things. i take everything personally and am constantly feeling attacked. when did i become so judgmental? when did i become so irritable? when did i become so hard to love? i breakdown at every opportunity; for a while it was out of my control. i've always been sensitive, but this is an entirely new level.

i have always put in too much effort. i've given too much. i've tried too hard. i've been taking for granted, and have been told my worst character trait is that i'm too nice. i let people walk all over me, take advantage of me, and expect things of me. i set myself up for this, and now i don't know how to go back. if i don't plan it, it won't happen. if i don't reach out, i won't hear from them. if i don't put in the effort our friendship will fail. why is it always on me?

i have a problem with control, and this is something i am aware of but i don't know how to change. i like knowing all of the details, having an idea of what to expect, and getting my way. i like knowing where my money is going, because i don't have hardly enough of it. i like making the plans so that i know it's within my means, and it'll include the people i wish to see and no one who makes me uncomfortable. i like that feeling of accomplishment, and being appreciated for my work. lately i haven't felt appreciated. lately i feel like everything is expected of me, and when it doesn't happen, i'm to blame. lately i've put too much pressure on myself.

i've feeling more regretful recently than i have in a very long time. if i could only go back...if i could only have done this, or that, i wouldn't be where i am today, i wouldn't be struggling and i wouldn't feel like i'm watching my whole world unravel. i know i can't change the past, i know that i can only move forward, i just need to find the motivation to keep moving forward, to put on those running shoes, to write that cover letter, to have that conversation. i need to be the one to decide to put that smile on my face, to stop taking everything so personally, to not let certain things impact me the way they have been. i need to be the one to decide when it's time to make things right, to make a change for the better, to take back the control of the one thing i should have full control over - my life. i have nothing to be so upset about.

i just need to believe it.

A couple of nights ago, I had, for the first time in years, a panic attack. I hadn't been feeling great about my anxiety for a while and it just all came to a head.

It starts as difficulty breathing, followed by an unbearable pain in my chest. Each muscle in my body intensely tightens and it is difficult for me to sit up straight. In between panicked breaths, I let out hoarse coughs that hurt my chest even more. No matter who is with me or how long I have struggled with this, no matter how much I learn or the different coping techniques I try, when a panic attack happens, the fear of dying is as real as it was during the first panic attack I had when I was in high school.

In short, it's chaos.

Within minutes of taking my anti-anxiety medication, I can feel my body start to calm down. After panic attacks, I feel exhausted and my body is really sore. I also feel this wave of sadness and defeat come over me. I feel complete disappointment in myself for losing control and I cry. It is safe to say that for at least the next 24 hours, I am not going to be myself. I am very hard on myself and that is something that I need to work on.

Yesterday was a really hard day for me. I struggle with the fact that this is just how I am wired and is something that I need to take care of for the rest of my life. I was thinking of writing an entry to the site but felt nervous to share this with everyone because it is not the usual uplifting stories I promote. But, I think it is important to tell the truth and for the people that read these posts to know that I continue to struggle—and that's okay. I think that it's important for me to realize that as well.

Writing out what happened and explaining in detail what goes on with me is my therapy. I know it sounds weird but I feel like some of the tension, anxiety and sadness is lifted from me when I just take my time and explain what is going on. Today is a much better day. I took care of myself yesterday and I have this awesome roommate who never runs for the hills when these things happen. I got some much needed rest and I feel almost back to myself today.

Life is never going to be smooth sailing. I continue to learn that every day. I am learning to cut myself some slack when I stumble. It is not a bad thing to breakdown from time to time and it is not defeat, it's life. We all need to continue to pick ourselves up afterwards and keep moving. It was just a bad day, not a bad life.

Jordan

Listen, Lucy,

"Strength does not come from winning. Your struggles develop your strengths. When you go through hardships and decide not to surrender, that is strength."

-Arnold Schwarzenegger

He was the one. THE one. I knew it from the moment I met him. He was charming, funny and drop dead gorgeous. The first night I met him, we talked until 4 o'clock in the morning. The very next day we took a walk in the park, he met my parents and soon became the gentleman that opened doors for me. Before I knew it, I was driving 4 hours to see him when he worked out of town, and was lavished with diamond jewelry, "just because." Months into the relationship, we decided to move in together. I kept thinking to myself, "This is it. This is the happiness that everyone always talks about." He knew the things I needed, before I knew I needed them. It wouldn't be for almost a year later, that I realized he knew exactly what I needed, because I no longer thought for myself.

Our relationship was great at the beginning. He worked out of town, so I kept a great balance with my friends and family. Then one day I decided I didn't want to go out anymore. Why would I go to bars when I already had the man of my dreams? Besides, the fight it would create the next day wasn't worth it.

I would see my family when he was out of town, and we would spend time with his family once he came home. I didn't mind always driving to go see his family, because he never saw them. Besides, the fight to stay in town wasn't worth it.

We stayed home and had quiet nights. I didn't mind not being social anymore because I adored the time we spent together. Besides, the fight to go out wasn't worth it.

My friends starting noticing the difference in the social, happy go lucky and fun friend they once had. They tried talking to me about it, but they didn't know what they were talking about--I WAS happy. I told my boyfriend about it, and he told me they were jealous and I didn't need jealous friends. Besides, the fight for their friendship wasn't worth it.

Weeks went on in my new world and I was happy and content. Around the holidays we decided to have some friends over for a small gathering and we both got drunk. I watched him whispering to a girl in the corner, right in front of me. I was crushed. I got upset and tried to talk to him about it. A broken bed, three holes in the wall and a door ripped off the hinges later, I realized I made a mistake. I was wrong to think he would ever do something like that in front of me. He would never do anything to hurt me. In turn, I would never do something so foolish to make him mad at me again, because the fight I created was not worth it.

I started to not live my life, but instead, one that was devoted to not making him upset. I was happy. I was numb. It was a relationship that I willingly stayed in. It was a relationship that I could not get out of.

I knew things started to really go wrong when I would get in trouble for not satisfying him sexually. I felt bad. I felt like a disappointment. I was told that if I didn't do it, he would find someone else who did. Before I knew it, I became THAT girl. And finally, I knew I wanted out.

I did it. I left. I found the strength to tell him that I was leaving, and

I was gone....for a week.

He missed me. He lost the best thing in his life. He didn't know how he was going to go on without me. He was in a bad place before, but he knew what he did wrong. He changed...and I believed it. After all we lived together, and I loved him. Our relationship deserved one last shot.

My parents, siblings and friends all told me he was just telling me what I wanted to hear. Yeah, right. What did they know? They weren't in the relationship. They didn't see him cry. They didn't know him like I knew him.. and maybe that was a good thing. I could lie to everyone else, but how much longer could I lie to myself? I, too, knew I was being the girl that believed everything he had to say, but I chose to believe it. I chose to ignore that pit in my stomach. I chose to ignore everyone I trusted that made me who I am today. I chose to ignore the (now patched up) holes in the wall. I chose to believe that things were going to work out because he was the exception.

My heart wanted to believe the world I created and ignored, but my head knew better. It took me a couple weeks and a public lashing later, but I finally listened to that sneaky little woman's intuition. It took me a little bit, but I finally found strength to be done.

Finally, the fight for ME was worth it.

Moving out was hard, but the people I didn't want to listen to for the past year made it that much easier. It was easy to lose sight of how much people cared about me when I was in the toxic relationship, but I learned quick that I have a good support system that will always be there for me. They knew someday I would find myself. I just needed to be the one to know what fight was worth it.

Listen Lucy,

Throughout the past calendar year I have seen too much tragedy occur. I have watched people that I love go through things that I never want them to go through. That's always the worst for me, seeing my loved one's go through things that are extremely trying. I have even gone through tragedy on my own and I can't say that I handled it with excellence, but life is about learning. When negative experiences occur it is easy to develop a negative outlook. However, that is not what this submission is going to be about.

A saying that I read on an earlier submission quoted a very intelligent man's famous saying, "Human beings are resilient". This quote really touched my heart and made me start thinking about how amazing human beings really can be. Even if you just look at the submissions on this site alone; an alcoholic who is beating his disease with confidence and determination, a newlywed couple losing their first child and instead of living with anger, carry out their daughter's legacy in the best way that they can, A young girl picks up the pieces after a break up and learned to love herself first, and a girl who has conquered her anxiety disorder and created this website as an outlet for those going through tough times to express themselves, in essence to read stories of other's resilience and find strength for themselves. This site breathes resiliency right off the screen and it got me thinking that amidst all the negativity around the world, there are incredible acts of courage, strength, resiliency, and heroism going on every single day.

In my life alone I see a family man of integrity lose his wife after sixty plus years of marriage. He cries, he is allowed to, he should. But every day he wakes up and continues not just her legacy, but their legacy.

I see a father who will do anything not just for his kids, but for anyone. His past is not perfect, no one's is. But every day he wakes up and works as hard as he can to improve himself, improve his wife and children's life, and the lives of the less fortunate.

I see a woman who is recovering from going into cardiac arrest that is only alive because of a miracle take care of her husband with dementia.

I see a mother who breaks her back for her children and her parents just to make sure that they're doing okay.

I see a young man recovering from two shoulder surgeries in five months, who has had his favorite thing in life taken away from him, show up to practice every single day with the same enthusiasm encouraging his teammates to be the best they can be.

You see, there is always going to be negativity surrounding you, such is life. But there is infinitely more good in the world than bad, I truly believe that. We just have to choose to see the fact that human beings are courageous. They can be mean, but mostly they are kind hearted. They are resilient for sure. They are amazing. Sometimes you just have to take a step back and really see it.

Listen Lucy,

I work with kids that are less fortunate than most. In most cases, they have been dealt a hand that most of us would pass on. They do what they can. They try in their own way. They get by. For them, it is one day at a time. They make mistakes, no doubt. Sometimes some very serious mistakes.

I wonder how I would do if I was in their shoes.

When I first meet them, there is usually resistance...not just from them. They have a look...an attitude. I try to think of a way to get past it. I know that it is going to take time. I have to be smart...be patient.

I wonder what they think about me.

They have a history of making poor decisions. I know this will continue to take place ...even in the future. Probably everyday.

Maybe it can happen less frequently.

One kid that I've worked with for a long time is in jail for a very serious charge. I really don't know if he did what he is accused of doing. But, I do know that at times he is a great kid. I know if I needed help, he would help me in a minute. I also know that he would do the same for a complete stranger. I really like this kid.

This scares me a little bit.

Another kid that I've worked with for years has a very difficult life.

He is also very poor. He lacks motivation and follow-through. This is evident everyday. I find myself getting very frustrated that he doesn't try harder. One day, he earned $10 on a part-time job. He used his $10 to buy a homeless man dinner.

I was not surprised by this.

There is another kid that I recently met. We haven't connected. He's tough. I know his story. It's not a good one. It's going to take more of an effort to connect. I just heard that while on a group visit to a library he found himself alone. He found a wallet laying on the ground that had, among other things, a substantial amount of cash in it. He turned it all in.

I have got to try harder.

Listen Lucy,

I have wonderful people in my life who never hesitate to tell me how smart, talented, beautiful and special I am … but I don't believe them. I hear the words and say the thank you's all the while thinking, "If you were me you wouldn't think so." It's not that I think I'm a terrible person, I know I am nice and pleasant but I'm average. Any time something amazing happens to me I chalk it up to luck, coincidence, or a blessing from God – nothing I did could have made this or that happen. My friends and family are always telling me to have more confidence, like I can just grab it out of thin air, but it's not that easy. As a child I think I was confident, I was definitely sensitive but I remember thinking I had strengths. I'm not sure when it all changed but I can feel the waves of insecurity and doubt rush over me almost daily, and then there's the guilt. Why do I feel this way when I have a loving family, the best friends and a caring and hilarious man who loves me? Surely something must be wrong with me if I can't feel good about myself with all the good that surrounds me. The place where it is currently affecting me the most is my career. I've never had a dream job or a goal I was aspiring to I just knew that I wanted to find something I could be happy doing and succeed. I always saw that as a negative, everyone has dreams and goals, where are mine? I have a good job where I am still pretty new and I try to work as hard as I can to prove myself. Still, no matter what, when my boss asks to speak with me I am positive I'm getting fired. I completely freeze, red face, sweating, tears welling up even after he tells me they are moving my position in order to preserve my spot in the company, it takes days for me to accept that he is telling the truth. I have an exciting life event coming up and as I prepare and receive gifts and congratulations, hearing how excited everyone is for me, I wonder why? There it is - the doubt. Always creeping up when I should be so happy and basking in everyone's enthusiasm for the big day. The interesting thing about it all is that most of the time, I am a happy person, I am just trying to figure out why I deserve the things I have. My hope is that with growing up I find peace with who I am and learn to accept the good things in my life for what they are. I truly am the luckiest girl in the world, I can't wait for the day I can see myself as others see me. That day will be awesome.

Listen, Lucy.

Have you ever been broken? Like really broken.. into what feels like a million tiny, little pieces? You're scared, hurt and angry because you think you'll never be able to find every little piece to put yourself fully back together again. First you blame everyone and everything you can think of, but then you realize it just comes down to you.. in reality, everything is your fault. What is so wrong with me that he didn't want me anymore? Why did he say the things he did? Did he mean any of it? Am I not pretty enough? Is there someone else? Every SINGLE possible question floods your mind every second of every day.

Some of you may be reading this thinking wow.. this girl got dumped.. big deal. Yes, I know there are plenty of people out there who have it MUCH, MUCH worse and would kill to have"problems" like mine. I can say that I am thankful that this is one of the biggest hardships I've been through in my life thus far. However, love IS the thing that makes the world go 'round. Love fuels every motivation, no matter if we realize it or not. If you're not in love, you're looking for love. If you're not looking for love, you're simply pretending you don't want it. Money and success can give you temporary joy, but material things merely can't give you true, permanent happiness.

I know, first hand, how powerful love is. I changed my ENTIRE life for love. I am so young, and I have so much potential; but I decided to put a guy before everything/everyone in my life, and now I have been left with what feels like nothing.

I have always had one goal in life: to get a kick-ass job that pays a lot of money. I wanted to prove to all of the people that have doubted me that I have more potential than they ever thought,and more importantly, I wanted the people I love to be proud of me. After working my ass off in college, I ended up turning down a great, very competitive job offer my first semester of my senior year. I decided I would keep looking because I knew love was more important. I wanted be married with a family, even if it was in a town with a population of 10,000. I did find a job, making 3x less money, in that tiny town. I graduated, moved here, and started my new "dream" job within 3weeks.

Everything was great for the first few weeks. I was so excited I finally got to see my boyfriend every day after being in a long-distance relationship for a year. I cherished waking up next to him and just doing everyday things like going grocery shopping. The simplest things like making him lunch or making his coffee in the morning made me smile. But my relationship suddenly fell apart.. within less than 2 months. We started fighting, a lot. He became obsessed with drinking with his friends more than he ever had. I quickly realized that his phone was much more interesting to him than I was. A complicated relationship with his sister, who was once one of my best friends, left me feeling inadequate and put on the back burner. Whenever I would confront him about my feelings, he would make me feel like I was wasting his precious time.

Suddenly, I started questioning every decision I ever made. I was living in an apartment all alone, and every person I knew in my new "home town" was either his friend or family. Then my biggest nightmare came true. After asking him why his priorities had seemed to change so much, I was presented with a response that I had feared for a while: He wasn't willing to compromise or work at this relationship any longer. He was done. We "mutually" agreed that we weren't right for each other, but I knew that I was losing the most important person in my life.. and to make it even worse, it was through a TEXT. He couldn't even bother to call me or come over to see me one last time. I left work early that morning and drove all the way home to my parents' house. The tears did not stop flowing.. for 3 days. When I came back to my lonely apartment, I completely broke down. I deleted every social media site I had so I wouldn't accidentally come across pictures of him happily carrying on with his life. I gathered his stuff together because I knew being reminded of him in any way would just kill me. I deleted every picture of him on my phone and threw away every piece of memorabilia in my apartment.

That following week was harder than I could have imagined. I was completely alone.. no family, and only a few friends who were carrying on with their own lives. I tried my best to be productive at work through the tears. I suddenly had so much free time, which meant more time for every crazy thought to enter my head. Hearing things like "he seems fine" and "he's already hanging out with his ex girlfriend" from his friends made me go completely crazy. Knowing that it took him less than a week to get over what I considered the most important relationship in my life beyond hurt me.. it destroyed me.

Here I am now, 2 weeks after the breakup, trying to pull myself together enough to merely function. I've been trying my hardest to take all of the advice everyone has given me to heart; but when it comes down to it, I just feel empty, lonely and numb. I can't eat, I can't sleep, and I can't get the memories of him out of my head. I am down to the lowest weight I have been in 5 years. I evoke every bad memory of the severe anxiety issues I faced when I was younger like it was yesterday, and I fear SO MUCH that my eating disorder is back again. It's so UNFAIR that I'm forced to be alone in this town with nothing to keep my mind off of him.

But, you know what? One thing I've learned is that LIFE IS UNFAIR. Feeling sorry for myself is going to get me nowhere.I can be sad and cry and think about the past as much as I want, but it's not going to change the way things are. I can give into my anxiety and depression liked I used to, or I can rise above it. After all, I have made my own decisions, and when it comes down to it.. it really IS my fault. I relied on one person for my happiness, and that's a lot of weight for one person to carry. I have to figure out how to love myself, and maybe being all alone is going to force me to do that for the first time in my life. You simply cannot rely on anyone.. for ANYTHING! Never depend on others. Rely only on yourself for your happiness because while other people can make it easier for you, only YOU can choose to be truly happy.

I know that I will never find EVERY piece of my broken self, because I have lost something that was such an important, significant part of me for so long. But I know that eventually, I will be able to find the biggest, most important pieces and maybe even some new ones that can fill in most of the empty spaces.

Listen, Lucy,

Drugs.

Grasping you.

Why can't you stop?

Why won't you stop?

Don't you want to stop?

Can't you see in my face that your hurting me?

Can't you tell your hurting yourself?

I choke back tears.

I want to cry.

I stay strong.

For you.

I can see you changing.

You body is different.

You don't talk much anymore.

I feel like you're no longer with me.

You ask for things.

Thats the only time we talk.

It hurts.

I want to cry.

I stay strong.

For you.

Years go by.

Don't you love me anymore?

Don't you miss me?

Your stare is blank.

Your body is weak.

I lose hope.

I cry.

I'm no longer strong.

Because of you.

I worry everyday.

Didn't you see the faces of those who died?

Not peaceful.

Gone too soon.

Never got to live.

I want you to die someday.

Old, satisfied, happy, sober.

Your soul is beautiful.

Sometimes I see it peaking through.

I hope it peaks through someday forever.

I'll tell myself to stay strong.

I'll put on a front.

I'll try not to cry.

I'll think of you everyday.

You will overcome this.

You will get better.

I will see the real you again.

I believe in you.

I'm your biggest fan.

I love you.

Listen, Lucy

Helplessness is horrible. When you are completely helpless in a situation there is no worse feeling. To watch someone you love deal with unbearable pain and not being able to stop it? There is nothing like it.

I have been witness to some horrible events in my life. Most of the time I was on the outskirts of the situation looking in on people I love trying to cope with a tragedy I couldn't understand. For a long time I tried to find reason as to why there is so much heart ache and pain and loss. I still don't have an answer. When I think of the sadness those closest to me have endured I feel a pit in my stomach. You try to find the right words to comfort them but there aren't any. There are no words to take away the pain of loss.

Unfortunately, this is life and it is hard. Horrible things happen and all you can do is be around to help your friends and family when they need it. You do not need to come up with the answers because there are no answers. You just have to be there. Be sturdy and responsible and reliable. Surround yourself with people you can count on. Surround yourself with people with loyalty because when a tragedy hits, those are the people who won't flinch. Be one of those flinch-less people.

When I was creating this site, I had a conversation with a couple of people about how much of the past I wanted to talk about and its importance to the success of this page. I felt like it was not important for me to get into the details, but to give an oversight as to what I went through. I am still overwhelmed by the support, kind words and amazing submissions to my project. I want to help people find their way through difficult times and I hope this site is doing that. What I didn't realize was how much it was going to help me.

A few weeks ago, I spoke at my old high school in a class where I sat and studied English. It was a really cool experience and it was my first time publicly speaking about *Listen, Lucy.* A lot of my issues started in that high school. I was sick and turned into a nightmare version of the lively teenager that I once was. It was one of the hardest times in my life and I always feel a pit in my stomach when I think back to high school, especially that year.

I spoke to the students about my past, how I got into writing, and why I wanted to create this site. I explained how alone I felt and how I would never wish that upon anyone. The teacher thanked me and I left the school feeling a bit of triumph. I was able to return to where it all started and speak about how I got through it. I didn't realize how important it was for me until a few days later.

I have worked really, really hard to get to where I am and sometimes I forget about how bad it was. I have tried to remain positive and I rarely let myself think back to those times but, really, working so hard to get healthy is why I am who I am (I learned this through one of the past entries on this site). It is also how I came about creating this site and now I have been able to read all of these stories and share them with my small world.

I promise you that it does get better. I am hoping someone that reads this post thinks, "I can get there."

I am not a huge success but I am happy and I am healthy and while I have a huge group of people to thank for helping me get there, the person I need to thank the most is myself—as cheesy as it may sound. I make no apologies for my past or the issues that I face day-to-day because we are all a work in progress. Progress is all you can ask for and, little by little, you have to keep working to get better. You will get there. You will also have your moment when you can look back on a crappy time in your life and see how far you have come and think, "I am awesome."

Jordan

Listen, Lucy,

I have never had any serious problems in my life. I have always been pretty confident,

I was a pretty popular kid in school, not that it would have even mattered to me if I wasn't. I never really cared what people thought of me. I have had amazing friends, friends I have had since kindergarten. I don't have many friends but the friends that I have are good ones. I have always been healthy. I have never had any issues getting a job. I actually one day said "I want to be an Event Planner" and I googled "Event Planners" in the area I was living in and I sent my resume and by the end of the week I was hired. I now have made a rather successful career for myself. Life seemed to just always work out for me ("knock on wood"). I have a really awesome family, I never really had any major family troubles aside from typical teenage issues. I was just always very lucky in life, I guess it was luck but whatever it was life just always seemed rather easy for me. I never worried about anything, if things didn't work out I just figured... oh well, things will work themselves out and I would move on. But the one thing that was always missing from my life was love. Not family and friends love but being that "knock it out of the ball park" kind of love, I always wanted that. Until about year ago I was beginning to think that perhaps I will never find it, maybe I have been given everything else in my life so easily, that maybe you really cannot have it all, maybe this will be my life...just me. And I was beginning to accept that. It took me 31 years to find the man I want to spend my life with and I will tell you it was worth every minute of waiting. June 9, 2012, one of my best friends text me asking if I was interested in going out with her friend's brother. June 10, 2012 he facebook inboxed me (thank you social media!). June 15, 2012 was our first date and I drove home from that date honestly thinking "Is it possible to throw up from feeling so happy?" I will never forget thinking that...it was the greatest. And we've been together ever since.

I wasn't sure what I wanted my message to be with writing this but then I realized, there are so many people out there that settle, that rationalize being with the wrong person just because they want to be with someone. I have been that person. I have been the person that puts the front up that you feel so happy but in your head you feel sad. I am here to tell everyone out there that settling should not be an option. You should not rationalize being with someone who does not make you over the moon happy, who does not love all of your flaws, who does not empower your decisions and support you. You should be with someone who when he/she looks at you, you can feel how proud they are of the person you are. You should be with someone who has your back. You should be with someone who looks at you when you feel so ugly and for some reason they shockingly tell you how beautiful you are. You should be with someone who makes it easy to work out your differences and you want to make it easy to work them out as well. I am here to tell you all... it is worth the wait. This is your life. You are in charge of your destiny and life is way to short to spend it with someone who does not appreciate you and who does not make you truly happy. Each and every one of us deserves to be happy, happier than we could have ever imagined. We all deserve to be content. Each and every day I feel so happy to come home just to see the smiling face of the man I love. I once read a quote that a friend posted who went through something so tragic in life and it stuck with me. The quote read "I'd rather have 30 minutes of wonderful than a lifetime of nothing special". I always kept this with me because that is how I always felt. You see all of these romantic love stories on tv and you think that is what you want, and to an extent that is what it is, only there isn't romance every day but just true joy and happiness that you feel inside. One of my girlfriends asked me a few weeks ago if I was just so excited for where my life is right now, and I explained that it doesn't feel the way I expected it to feel. I am not jumping out of my skin and wanting to run around like a crazy person screaming from rooftops but I just feel incredibly content and at ease...and I'll tell you...that feeling is the very best feeling in the world. Life can be so crazy and so tragic and so dramatic and so sad and so stressful and so hurtful at times...to feel at ease and content and happy....well there isn't anything better in my opinion. So for all of you people out there who are feeling in your head like you are settling but are trying so hard to rationalize it...I am living proof...I am here to tell you..there is something, someone, better out there for you. Someone who is your someone who will make all of your days brighter and better and happier...you just have to be strong enough to wait for them to arrive.

Listen, Lucy,

I always thought life shouldn't be this difficult. I have always worked hard, my husband works extremely hard every day. I was always told told if you work hard good things will come to you. After many, many years of working hard I thought I should have more, be able to go on vacation once in a while, be able to buy the things I want and so on. I can't buy things I want, I can't go on vacation and I didn't know why. A few months ago I read a passage in a book , God said, I gave you everything you truly need. God is never wrong so I guess I was looking in all the wrong places and just maybe I do have everything I need.

Listen, Lucy –

Loss is loss. It never gets easier. It never goes away…

She was doing what she loved. She was enjoying a beautiful Sunday morning in Chicago. She had just returned from a trip to China. She was planning her retirement and her move back to her beloved Pittsburgh. That return to Pittsburgh did happen, but not the way that she had planned. It was on that Sunday morning that our lives were changed forever. It was later in the evening that we learned what had happened and it was the first time in my life that I truly knew what loss was. I knew what grief was and what hate was. I had never been so angry in my life. I was sixteen years old and I had just lost one of the women that I admired most. She was struck and killed by two men who were coming home from a bar. They had probably been drinking all night. They lost complete control of their van, drove up onto a curb, and killed my aunt. We have had some tragic deaths in our family, but we never thought we'd lose her this way. I remember my dad and his siblings travelling to Chicago in the days after and I remember hoping and praying that they had the wrong woman…

This happened in July 2002. It seems as if it happened yesterday. The pain and the anguish are still present. Every holiday, every wedding, every family vacation, there is a void. She is not there. The sun rises and sets everyday, whether or not we believe it is going to do so. I knew that my life would never be the same and it is not. But looking back, I have grown stronger and I now see some good that came from the bad.

Right before her trip to China, I had reconstructive knee surgery. My dad was out of town and my mom had four children to take care of. My aunt came to the rescue. She drove from Chicago, probably listening to books on tape the entire way (I never knew how she could do it and not fall asleep). We spent an entire week together, I learned things I never knew, and I grew to admire her on a level I never had before. She quizzed me on SAT questions and she told me time and time again that I could do whatever I put my mind to. I realized what a classy, intelligent, humorous, and genuinely compassionate person she was. She had a heart of gold, yet she always told you exactly what she thought (whether you were going to like it or not). God gave me that week with her; a week that I cherish more than anything.

Recently, with the loss of another friend to a tragic accident, I believe I have finally found some solace and some peace. I believe that everything happens for a reason. I trust in God and I trust that these loved ones have been taken from this life for a reason. I know that they are in a better place. I know that they are happy. Life goes on. They would not want me to be sad. They would want me to remember the good times (and there were SO many good times). At my dear friend's funeral, I was reminded of his humor and I was consoled by something that he had written in our eighth grade yearbook. His favorite song 'Tears in Heaven' by Eric Clapton reminded me that, "beyond the door, there's peace I'm sure, and I know there'll be, no more tears in heaven".

Listen Lucy,

I am a husband, a father, a son, and a brother. I am a godfather, an uncle, a cousin and a friend. I am also an alcoholic.

The very first time I said those words I was nervous. I wasn't sure I could do it. I was in a room full of strangers and I didn't know what to expect or how I would be received. Each meeting the words came out a little easier. Now I look back on those days and I realize just how therapeutic they were. For me, saying these words was humbling and at the same time provided me with a sense of freedom.

Presently, I worried about putting these words to text, but after I had time to think about it, I knew it was the right thing to do. Anyone who knows me well, is aware of my situation and, for the most part, understands. My initial worry about writing it down was that others would judge me, unjustly. Then, I realized this is who I am. The accumulation of my past experiences makes me, me. Besides, I think this is what Listen Lucy is all about --- being able to express yourself freely in hopes that if others are out there experiencing the same types of issues, they can find comfort in seeing that they are not alone.

Without going into specifics and without minimizing the effect of my disease, my troubles with drinking were pretty typical to others that experience problems with alcohol. I was never able to control it. Generally, when drinking, I would consistently make poor decisions that I normally would not make. I didn't get in any "severe" trouble, but that was because I was fortunate. It could have been much, much worse. My health suffered. But the biggest problem wasn't that I was hurting myself, it was I was hurting the people that were most important to me.

It was difficult to finally understand and admit that, for me, alcohol was the problem. Once I finally admitted it, I knew I could do something about it. I knew where to go. I am not deeply religious, but I knew my recovery had to begin with prayer. For the first few months, I went to mass every day and prayed for strength to overcome my problem. God gave me the strength and showed me the way. I went to meetings and learned how others can listen and be open-minded. I distinctly remember another person's advice to the group while sharing his thoughts, "Slow down, get in the slow lane and go the speed limit." For some reason, these words stuck with me; they gave me hope. I pursued counseling. I talked and listened. Days turned into weeks and weeks turned into months.

August 8, 2013 will be 7 years of being clean and sober. My health has improved, but more importantly so has my perspective. I feel things now that I had never felt before. In many ways, I feel like a new person. I really like this feeling. I have a long way to go, but feel as though I am closer to becoming the person that I want to become.

I never want to drink again. I feel pretty confident that I will be successful with this goal. But, from what I've learned, I know that becoming too confident can be dangerous. I realize that for the rest of my life, I will always have to guard against becoming too confident.

I am a husband, a father, a son, and a brother. I am a godfather, an uncle, a cousin and a friend. I am also an alcoholic.

My dearest Listen Lucy,

This is the first time I've put any of this to pen, and I am doing it for a reason that I hope is more beneficial to others than to myself. I don't want to write to share my struggles – instead, I hope that this shines some light on the brilliant perspective of recognizing the good that does exist and making the most of your life…really taking advantage of the YOLO! Unfortunately, you will have to bear through my struggles to reach my happiness!

13 months and 29 days ago, my world turned upside down. I was diagnosed with a chronic condition that I that be apart of me every day for the, next 76 years – yes, I have every intention to live until I am 100 years old! After my diagnosis I was put on medicine that did not agree with my system at all, to the point that 16 days later I found myself in the hospital with doctors poking and prodding every inch of my body–trying to figure out exactly what was happening internally. I was living my very own episode of HOUSE, but I was the patient (in my mind I always play House, he is brilliant and British – does it get much better?!). I faced a choice, as I lay in bed surrounded by IVs, my rock of a mother and doctors contemplating what my next step would be. Nearly finished with my first year in graduate school, my mom gave me the choice of continuing my program or taking a well-needed, long break.When my mom, the woman who wouldn't let me watch tv or talk on the phone until my homework was finished growing up, said this I knew I had a trying road ahead of me. I made the decision in seconds – recognizing

that quitting a graduate school I spent four years trying to get into was not an option – I NEVER have believed in giving up on dreams for any reason.

For months I struggled every single day. I was forced to watch every single piece of food I put into my mouth, monitor the way my body felt every single hour of the day, take a combination of pills, ointments, and self-injections and more frequently than not I couldn't control my tears. For me, my condition was extremely unique as I never fit the stereotype and while I feel great, my insides are at a constant war, leaving specialists at a loss and me extremely frustrated. As things began to shape up and I got my quality of life back, my condition came back with a vengeance. Between January and February I was given news that rattled me worse than my initial diagnosis. My method of coping was spending the next 14 days laying on my couch feeling (and definitely looking) like death (it was not attractive, probably even a little bit scary), as I took medication that knocked the light out of me. I hit rock bottom, no doubt. My mom, making the four-hour drive, found me on the couch of my apartment, unable to stop crying and unable to grasp that I am a resilient and strong young woman. I couldn't understand what I had done to deserve the path that I was given – I worked hard everyday, I was nice, I took care of my body, I never ate junk food, I worked out, I went to church and my family and friends were so loved. I, in a moment of regretted weakness blamed God and felt betrayed. And, this time I didn't know how to pick myself back up and I was too proud to ask professionals for help.

The thing about rock bottom though, is there's only way to go: UP. I had two choices: to feel sorry for myself, which I never have, or to actually LIVE. I cant say at which point I made my decision but I can promise you it was someone who made me laugh very hard one day that changed everything. My world is rife with complications but guess what? Everyone has their own set of problems – andmy problems, or yours, are no worse than someone else's – even when it seems like the darkest, gray cloud is hovering over only you (solution: find a giant, by giant I mean GINORMOUS, umbrella a.k.a a support system). In fact, I count myself to be one of the lucky ones – a blessed soul. So I began to live. I lived each day – I threw away the rules that were so strict I stopped living in the first place, and most importantly I found things that made me laugh- I've been told it is the best medicine around! I realized that I had a group of ROCKSTARS for my support and among them the incredible person that pulled me out of my slump (little did I know until just recently, I pulled him out of his!).

Now it is May, and exactly 14 months and 6 days after my diagnosis I will graduate with my master's degree and begin my professional career 5 days later. Looking, back I couldn't be happier (in fact I am certain it was recognizing this as my greatest goal that landed me my AWESOME new job!).

So to all of Listen Lucy's readers, here's some perspective for your struggles that helps me: When my life feels like its the worst of the worst, I think back to my run-ins at the hospital, and how every time I am there I feel so sad for the person in the room next to me, and so happy to be me. I remind myself that I am not being punished but simply this is a PART of my life –NOT MY LIFE; but rather, an occasional hiccup that reminds me to be humble and thankful for everything I have- #faithrestored (still apologizing to God on that one). Look around and recognize that tears are not a sign of weakness but that those tears represent your faith that 'it has to get better' and you will not settle for anything less, be patient to those around you because you have no idea what they woke up to that morning and most importantly remember that not everyday is a rainy day- there will be bad but it is always counteracted with good.

Today: I live more colorfully, I smile more frequently and love more deeply.

Remembering this, I go back to the life that consumes all of me, the life of a 20 something female, done with school, living in an urban city, an exciting career ahead and complaining about the fact that my 'incredible' lives on a different continent. Now that my friends, is one of my biggest problems, my other half is an ocean away: #firstworldproblems!

Listen, Lucy

I often forget how lucky I am. I come from an amazing group of family and friends. I'm beautiful, athletic, funny, and have a personality that lights up a room. There are so many things I love about myself, and I'm not afraid to admit that—but I wasn't always like this. In fact, I had to go through the most devastating heartbreak to acquire the love I have for myself today. Here is my story.

I dated someone for 4 years. It was a very healthy relationship and everyone close to us would have said the same. But when he decided to break it off, my entire world stopped. Literally, I stopped. I could not understand what was so wrong with me. I could not stop texting him, begging for him back. I could not stop contacting his family, hoping to still feel connected to him somehow. I felt so weak and helpless. I couldn't eat. I couldn't sleep. I couldn't study. I couldn't talk without crying. I lost 20 pounds and failed 3 exams. I told my parents I didn't want to go back to school the next semester. I had no idea who this girl was. One night at school, I was sitting in my apartment alone. I picked up my phone, and texted my mom something so disturbing that almost NO ONE knows about. I was questioning whether or not I wanted to live, without him in my life.

The next morning, I received an E-mail from my dad, and I want to share some of it with you:

"I have been staying pretty neutral through all of this, because that's just me, but I just can't anymore. I knew the day would come when one of you decided to try flying solo. It happens. I also knew that you were not the one to ever believe this, so why bother telling you. When I heard about it, I felt very sorry for you, but I was happy too. These are the things that help us grow. YOU have to figure a way to be without him. Nobody can help you. They can comfort you. They can point you in the right direction. They can write you stupid emails or texts, but YOU and only YOU have to pull it together and start walking again, AND you need to do it for YOU and not for anyone else. Life is not and never should be about any one person. If he is the only thing that defines you as a person, then that is a relationship you should not be in anyway. I don't believe that, and I don't think you believe that, because you, of all people, have so much!! More than most people. You better believe that. You are not perfect, but you are pretty damn close to it, but sitting still and being numb because you cannot figure a way to be without him is not who YOU are. You are not that person. You are someone that is so touched by the world. That is a beautiful way to be. I wish I was more like you, and I try to be. You care!! You give a shit!! I love that about you. You get that from your mom. Ok ... I am done. You are wonderful. He is a fool. And love ...... well ..... it's undefinable and fleeting. It is the best drug and the worst poison all at the same time. I say figure out a way to love yourself, love your life, and the hell with anyone or anything that stands in your way.

I love you .... more than you will ever know .... Dad"

This is only half of the E-mail, but I read this E-mail EVERY single day. It has been a year and a half since my heart was broken, and I still read this every day. Not so much because I need it still, but because this is the E-mail that essentially saved my life. I have absolutely no idea where I would be without my dad. This man has taught me so much about not just love, but life. He is the smartest guy I know. I have never been so strong in my entire life. NOTHING can upset me now. NO ONE can hurt me now. I am more independent than I ever thought I could be. I was numb for about an entire year after the breakup. I stopped crying every day, but I did not stop thinking about it. It wasn't until these past 6 months that I am now 100% ready to move on and it feels amazing. I know I am worthy and I know I have the ability to make someone else happy. Not every love story ends in a happily ever after…but sometimes it ends to teach you that you are stronger than you ever thought possible. I am the STRONGEST girl I know and I truly believe that.

He will never know how much he affected my life.

He will never know how strong I am now.

But that doesn't matter.

As long as I know, and as long as I love myself, I win.

Listen, Lucy,

I was born and raised in a city, community, and family where football is king. In a way, football has been my life for as long as I can remember. I used to wake my parents up at six in the morning every Sunday just so I could look at the newspaper to see the football helmets; football is actually how I learned how to read. I could do multiplication by seven by kindergarten because that's how much a touchdown is worth. I loved everything about the game, and my life revolved around it. In fact, I am going to school to become a teacher and a football coach.

Growing up in a family where football is so often talked about only made my love for the game grow. We played it at every family function and it dominated conversation at every holiday. God forbid someone try to have a wedding during football season, that's grounds to call off the wedding. I grew up watching my cousins, and especially my brother, play for our high school team and have amazing success. I worshiped my brother and wanted to be just like him, this meant that I HAD to be a great football player, no excuses at all. Coming from a community and family where football is so dominant, my mind was brainwashed to think that I had to start as a sophomore, I had to make all-conference, I had to make All-star teams, because in my mind that's all that really mattered. I couldn't have been more wrong.

When I came to college I had that same attitude, I had to start as a freshman, and if I didn't, I better start by the time I was a sophomore or I will be too embarrassed to show my face around the community. Well guess what happened. I didn't start as a freshman or a sophomore, and I let this game that used to be the love of my life, become my biggest stressor and allowed it to cause me grief instead of joy. I was depressed, there is no other way to describe it. That's when I had the conversation with my dad that changed my views on life forever. He told me, "I think this is the year that you are going to start, but, if you don't, who really cares it's just a game." It was here that the words that I had heard for so long and had chosen to ignore had finally sunk in. Football is just a game! At the end of the day does it really matter what you did on the football field? Forty years from now will anyone remember or care what kind of football player you were? I hope not.

Instead of a life revolving around football I have chosen to live a life dedicated to helping others. I love the fact that I am going to become a teacher because it means that every single day I have an opportunity to change the world, to make someone's life a little better. At the time I decided I wanted to be a teacher, it was mainly because I wanted to be a high school football coach. Yes, I do still want to coach football, but now for all the right reasons. As a coach I will have the chance to work with kids who were in the same position that I was in. Day in and day out I will be able to relate to them and preach that is important to be the best football player you can be, but it's infinitely more important to be the best person that you can be.

Have you ever heard the phrase "Football is life", I used to live by that. It turns out I wasn't really living at all. When it comes down to it, football, shopping, work, whatever it may be, doesn't really matter. What really matters is if you're making the world a better place every day. I probably won't make it to the Pro Football Hall of Fame, but that's okay, I'm just going to keep trying to make people smile.

Listen Lucy,

I am my own worst enemy. I have mentally and emotionally beaten myself up for far too long. We are all human. We all make mistakes. That is what growing up is all about. I will forgive myself. I will pray for strength. I will come to terms with my past. I've knocked myself down, but I'm going to get back up. I'm going to tune out all of the things that tell me I'm the mistakes I've made because I know that's not true. I will not let an event in my past overcome who I am and define my being. Sometimes things in life really make you wonder. I know this event was thrown at me for a reason. As cliché as it sounds I believe in that motto. My past was a lesson and it has allowed me to realize that it's okay to cry sometimes; even if your problems aren't as serious as someone else's. Crying is my therapy. Crying has helped me drain my emotions. But I don't want to cry anymore. I will conquer this and I will be happy again. Thank you Lucy.

She showed us that it is possible to fall in total, complete and unconditional love with one person and to feel that love grow every single day of your life together. She lived a full life with the person she loved most in the world and created this enormous, loving army of a family and that is the legacy of their love story that will live on forever. She taught us how to love with everything we have.

As I plan my own wedding to the love of my life, I feel a void. I miss her smile and laughter. I wish I could have seen her reaction to my engagement and I wish she could be there to see me in my wedding dress. It is a type of missing that I have never felt before. While I understand that this is a part of life and that I was lucky enough to have her around through 25 years, the feeling of loss and sadness still sometimes sneaks up on me while I am thinking about my wedding, my future, and the life I want to build with my fiancé.

Her love story with my pap is one for the ages and one I will share with my children. It is a perfect example of what love should be, what marriage should be. I know on my wedding day there will be something missing and I know my entire family will feel it. I also know that she will be watching over us while I walk down the aisle, when we sing our song and while we dance in celebration of a new marriage—one that will hopefully be as special and as meaningful as her's and my pap's.

GramZ was the essence of love and laughter. Her joy is something that really is in each of us and if we continue to pass her joy, her memory, and her being on to our children and our children's children—if we try to emulate the life she lived and the marriage she had—will she ever truly not be around? I feel the void of her not being with us, but I know she is never too far away.

Jordan

Listen Lucy,

I must admit, life has been somewhat kind to me throughout my years on this earth. I have been fortunate to have a good family, good friends, a place to call home, and food on the table. After 25 years, I am able to say that life has treated me well and if I had to do it all over again, I would. While this has been the case most often, I have had my share of daily struggles and seemingly overwhelming obstacles to conquer. Each time a new struggle comes up, it seems more monumental than the last. However, I am extremely aware that the magnitude of my struggles may not even come close to those of another. From an empathetical standpoint, I think my suffering has given me the opportunity to acknowledge and relate to another during their times of grief, pain, and sadness, even if I have never "walked a mile in their shoes". What it boils down to though, really, is the importance of everyone's feelings during their times of hardship. I firmly believe that it is important to validate someone's hardship and not to diminish their suffering in comparison to another. What I am trying to say is that the obstacles in my life have generated suffering, pain, sadness, and grief, even if the magnitude of that suffering is different from another. So the question remains: how do I cope? For me, running has always been my outlet.

I entitled this "Why I Run" because I think it is important to determine why we do the things we do for stress relief, fun, and overall general health. By trial and error, I learned that running, more so than anything else, was most beneficial for me during times of stress, boredom, anger, or unhappiness. There are many ways to alleviate tension, some people talk to a therapist, write in a journal, listen to music, or even read a good book to just unwind from the hardship of our daily struggles. Aside from running, I find music and writing to be exponentially helpful in the healing process. I have been fortunate enough to have the capacity to use my body in a way that allows me to enjoy nature (all by my lonesome) while exercising and sometimes, even listening to loud music. This to me has been the perfect way to de-stress.

I write this to express my passion about running during some of the most difficult times in my life, and even still, some of the happiest. I have suffered from heart-ache, rejection, humiliation, family crises, school difficulties, work drama, and overall stress, just like the rest of us. "A healthy lifestyle" was modeled to me as a kid but in some cases, not followed through by those modeling it. Lack of communication has permeated relationships in my life, to a point where the relationship came to an end, and suffering ensued. I have lost loved ones due to death and friends to drugs. These hardships have shaped me as an individual. In order to deal with them, running became a way of life, a way to get my body moving, clear my mind, and be creative with my thoughts. It has generated more pleasure than anything else.

Being alone in nature while running is the most therapeutic aspect of the sport, or at least for me it is. It gives me time to refocus my energy on something other than my problems, on something other than another person, or another situation. It allows me to clear my mind and activate a part within me that generates drive, ambition, and determination; but still be creative enough to generate problem-solving ideas. For a while, and even still today, running is difficult. It takes energy from my entire body to keep moving and pushing forward. Some days it's easy to run and some days it is much more difficult. On the days when it is difficult, or I am tired, hungry, fatigued, or exponentially frustrated, I have to find a reason to keep going. I do this because this is my outlet and I know that if I can get past that next mile in nature, I can get past anything that "real life" throws me.

Aside from activity, quotes, passages, meditation, and reading have helped me to calm my anxieties or worries. A favorite quote of mine, from author William James, sums it all up: "Beyond the very extreme of fatigue and distress, we may find amounts of ease and power we never dreamed ourselves to own; sources of strength never taxed at all because we never push through the obstruction". I always try to remember this when faced with a difficult decision or when running in nature. It has helped me to keep pushing forward, even in the face of hardship.

Thank you for giving us a place to express ourselves creatively, Lucy. :)

Listen, Lucy.

My experiences in life have been somewhat disheartening. From the time I was born until the day I said no more, I was told I had a learning disability. I had a speech impediment that made me sound dumb and dyslexia that made me skink at reading out loud. My courage was buried so deep within my mind that even I couldn't find it. That was until the day I realizes that the only thing that entombed my courage was the people saying I was dumb and separating me from the normal kids. I realized that I had the power to exhume my shattered spirit. I put aside the thoughts of the people that were trying to "help" me with ridicule and dumbed down learning. I wanted to prove to them that I could be better without them taking credit for it. I started to read my books, to challenge myself, and to say what I have and what I didn't have. From that day on I didn't have a learning disability because I didn't let a single person tell me I did. Now I am taking my seventh AP class, accepted to all of my colleges, and using some pretty good resurrection imagery in the first couple of sentences. My friends and I have a thing we do when things are not going our way. We hold are hand up and pull on an in visible truck horn. It's a message to us that if something gets in the way it's that things problem to get out of the way. Nothing can stop a truck if you keep the gas on. That is the only way to truly get over problem, do it yourself and don't let anyone tell you what you can or cannot do. That goes especially for those who are pushed down by a person who thinks they know you better than you do.

Listen Lucy,

My struggle is actually happening now; during my senior year. I am in a Trigonometry and Pre-Calculus class and from the very beginning of this class I have been struggling to keep a passing a grade. I started with a B but when our chapter tests started coming my grade started to drop drastically. Ever since elementary school i have had problems understanding math. There has been one year, my eleventh grade year, that I have truly understood it. I ended my eleventh grade math class, which was Algebra 2 with a high B. My teacher was so good at explaining and breaking down the problems for me. I don't know how to deal with my class now though. I ask questions and get extra help outside of class but grade still remains low. I already am going to a good college so that is not an issue but for my own sake i would like to know I passed this class safely, not with a barely passing grade. I'm still going to try my hardest to work through the struggle of my of math and hopefully I will receive the best outcome!

Listen, Lucy,

I am not lonely

I am just alone.

And sometimes I like it

And other times I don't.

I am a big girl and I can be by myself.

But there are times where I feel like a prisoner of my own mind.

& I can't leave the monsters that inhabit it behind.

I run away from my past

But some how the memories always seem to last.

Time heals most things, but not all

Cuts, scrapes, and hearts but maybe no what happened that fall.

The pain sinks in and I can't push my demons aside

They crawl inside of me and ask to take over and I must abide.

Then they stop and disappear and I am okay,

That is until they come back the next day.

I am not lonely

I am just alone.

And sometimes I like it

And other times I don't.

I am a big girl and I can be by myself.

Listen, Lucy

Like most people I've had my deal of struggles throughout my life. I don't claim to have it any better or worse. I don't strive for pity nor to I condone receiving it, but one thing that I'll focus on that I have been dealing with most of my life is anger issues. To put it simply, I can not control it. I've gotten better over the years and what has helped me is finding my girlfriend. Is the past I have had my little melt down and rampages where I've put holes on the walls and broke stuff but I'm getting better...well in the process of it anyways. I've gotten to an age where I can wrap my head around how stupid inflicting self harm is, its just when I use to snap it seemed to be the easiest option. A few broken bones and stitches are all that really remind me of how bad it was and how upset I use to get, but now when I feel to upset I just think of the girl I care for and it manages to calm me, relatively speaking. All in all, I feel that through positive thinking and hard work I'll be able to better control any flares of rage I get. Thank you so much for hearing me out and this website sounds like a great idea!

Listen Lucy,

I'm a senior in high school and i have become very stressed out. On top of playing two sports, I have to keep up my GPA, apply to colleges, and make some big decisions that can affect my life majorly. This year has made me realized that things aren't going to be much easier once I go into college. Making a decision on where to go is so hard because there are so many things effecting my decision. These factors are my parents, location, reputation, size, etc. I feel that only being 17 I shouldnt have to make this kind of decision by myself. Yes I do have my parents and counselors helping me make my decision, but in the end it's all up to me. I feel so pressured when making my decision because of how expensive college is and if I don't like it I could have potentially wasted thousands of dollars. I am starting to close is on my decision, but I find it hard to make sure I'm doing the right thing for myself. I feel like it would be a lot easier to make a decision if there weren't so many options. I have gotten into a school in their honors program but no sports. i got into another school to play a sport there but no honors program, so in the end it comes down to if I want to play the sport or not. In the end I think I'm going to play the sport but i don't know if it is better to go for academics. All in all, senior year is not the blow off year that I was hoping for. Even though I am maintaining my GPA, sports, work, and a social life. This is one of the most stressful times for me right now.

Listen, Lucy

The pain lingers with me everywhere I go

You were taken away and never brought back

You never got to live, and I wonder what you'd be like

I know you're in a better place, even if it's not here with me

You were taken away and never brought back

You became an angel with beautiful wings

I know you're in a better place, even if it's not here with me

But I still wonder why I never got to say goodbye

Listen, Lucy.

Together Forever

My best friend, my love, my laughter

we were inseparable but after,

He moved away, we talked no longer,

those few months our love grew stronger.

The letters written came and went,

at the mailbox is where my time was spent.

I waited for him to come home

to let him know he's not alone.

Being thousands of miles apart is rough

I'm always asked, how do you do it?

I say, it's tough.

I know soon we'll be together

but for now I will weather.

Through the hurt I keep my head tall

so my heart will never fall.

I love my Marine no matter where we are

and I know he's here whether near or far.

Listen, Lucy,

Pretty soon I'm headed off to college. I've always grown up with a very tight-knit family, even through the divorce when I was 12. Recently I learned that my dad is planning on moving from the house I've grown up in for my whole life to be with his girlfriend and her kids. I'm torn because my house has so many memories with it, and my dad just doesn't understand that. I want him to be happy, but when I come home from college I want to be able to come home; not to a strange new house. I told my dad that my decision was to not live with him in his new house because his girlfriend and her kids are not my family. I told him I'd visit occasionally too but I just don't want to stay there. My dad isn't one to wear his heart on his sleeve, so it was very strange to see him cry when me and him went out to dinner. I'm feeling a mix of emotions and don't know what to do at this point. My dad was always my best friend and over time we've started to grow apart. I don't want to shut him out of my life, but I've barely been around his girlfriend and she's a stranger to me. I don't want to hurt my dad's feelings but I also don't want to put myself in an awkward situation. I've only talked to my mom and grandma about this and don't usually vent to people I don't know, but this actually helps. I used to keep a journal just so I could get my emotions out in the open so I wouldn't bottle them up until I got to my breaking point. So thank you for listening. It means a lot.

Listen, Lucy.

I have been dealing with a lot of grief as I count down the days till my high school graduation; which is suppose to be a happy event. I can relate much of this grief to what occurred about eleven years ago, when my father passed away from cancer. As the days go by and I grow older each day I find it harder to coupe with the fact that my father will not be here to witness all that I have accomplished in life, as well as my accomplishments to come. Even though, I know he would be extremely proud on the young woman I have grown to be, every girl dreams of and appreciates her father being by her side. However, his absence encourages me each day to accomplish something new. I strive to be the best and to achieve the highest because I know he is looking down on me and pushing me along the way. I used to be so angry that he was taken from me. However, now I see that even though he is gone from my sight, he will always be there to encourage me. From here on out, I would like to devote my life accomplishments to my father. Regardless of the fact that he will not be there to cheer me on, I know he is in heaven with a proud heart.

Listen, Lucy,

I am strong and determined.

I wonder about the future.

I hear my kids laughing.

I see my wedding day.

I want to have a good job.

I am strong and determined.

I pretend I am rich.

I feel proud of my accomplishments.

I touch the diploma in my hand.

I worry about messing up.

I cry for failure.

I am strong and determined.

I understand I must work hard.

I say that I have to fight for what I want.

I dream that everything goes my way.

I try to do my absolute best.

I hope for a successful and long life.

I am strong and determined.

Closing Message

Listen, Lucy is about creating a less judgemental, more accepting world. I hope this book helps to accomplish that. While reading these stories, I hope you took notes, dog-eared pages, used highlighters and screenshot different sections of different stories that have impacted your life. I hope it helped you heal. Each person is going to get something different out of what they just read. That is what makes *Listen, Lucy* so cool.

When I first started all of this, I just wanted to help someone who was struggling like I struggled. I had no idea how much this was going to teach me. I have learned that to struggle means something different to each person, but it is something we all face in our lives. I have come to realize that life is hard and people are resilient. The proof is on every single page of this book. *Listen, Lucy* has showed me how much people are going through but that they are able to remain positive and find the good. It has become clear that, as judgemental and difficult as the world can be at times, there are so many people out there that want to make it positive and who want to help each other. I have also learned that people need support. It does not matter whether this support comes from friends, family, coworkers or the complete strangers that read *Listen, Lucy*. None of us want to feel alone. All of us want to feel heard. Everyone has a story.

Unfortunately, passing judgement is human nature. It is our natural instinct. My goal with sharing these stories is to help people accept and respect each other and make this world a happier, brighter place to be. I hope something in this book lit a spark in you. I hope it helps you to accept yourself and the life you have been given. I hope it gives you courage to tell your story. If so, feel free to tell me about it at *Listen, Lucy*.

Cheers,

Jordan

35000030R00101

Made in the USA
Middletown, DE
15 September 2016